HOW *to* USE

Microsoft®
Access 2000

Pamela Rice Hahn
Keith Giddeon

201 W. 103rd Street
Indianapolis, Indiana 46290

SAMS

Visually in Full Color

How to Use
Microsoft® Access 2000

International Standard Book Number: 0-672-31589-0

Library of Congress Catalog Card Number: 98-87628

Printed in the United States of America

This book was produced digitally by Macmillan Computer Publishing and manufactured using computer-to-plate technology (a film-less process) by GAC, Indianapolis, Indiana.

First Printing: July 1999

01   00   99   4   3   2   1

Trademarks

Warning and Disclaimer

Acquisitions Editor
Randi Roger

Development Editor
Alice Martina Smith

Managing Editor
Lisa Wilson

Project Editor
Rebecca Mounts

Copy Editor
Sean Medlock

Indexer
Mary Gammons

Proofreader
Mary Ellen Stephenson

Technical Editor
Susan Harkins

Interior Design
Nathan Clement
Aren Howell

Cover Design
Nathan Clement
Aren Howell

Copy Writer
Eric Borgert

Layout Technicians
Brandon Allen
Stacey Richwine-DeRome
Timothy Osborn
Staci Somers

Contents at a Glance

Table of Contents

About the Authors

Pamela Rice Hahn has been writing about computers for over 13 years, during which time she's published more than 200 articles. However, she has worked with computers since her college days back in the punch-card era, circa 1969.

Pam is the 1997 winner of The Manny Award for Nonfiction from the MidWest Writers Workshop. She served as an editor for a number of computer-related and business newsletters, and has ghost-written articles that have appeared in *Glamour*, *Country Living*, and other national publications.

Pam can often be found as Fawnn during her Virtual Water Cooler breaks on the Undernet chat channel, #Authors, where she is channel manager. Stop in; she'll gladly tell you about the MBABGDITW—Most Beautiful and Brilliant Grandaughter in the World—and the MHABGSITW—Most Handsome and Brilliant Grandson in the World. (Pam points out that she was a young bride and therefore is a *very* young grandmother; her only child, a married daughter, Lara, works as a nurse and is a published author as well.) Look for the #Authors site Web pages, designed by Keith Giddeon, at http://www.blueroses.com/authors/. Pam can be reached by email at fawnn01@bright.net.

In addition to technical writing and editing work on numerous books and articles, Pam is coauthor with Dr. Dennis E. Hensley of *Writing for Profit*. Pam and Keith Giddeon cowrote *Master the Grill the Lazy Way* (Macmillan General Reference) and design and edit an online magazine, *The Blue Rose Bouquet*, at http://www.blueroses.com. Pam's Web site is at http://www.ricehahn.com.

Keith Giddeon writes and edits computer books on HTML, Web development, and office applications. He lives in Pensacola, Florida, where he owns a Web design and consulting business in addition to his writing and editing projects.

To learn more about him and his work, visit Keith's Web site at http://www.giddeon.com/.

Acknowledgements

Pam and Keith would like to thank **Randi Roger** for her belief in our abilities that made us the right team for this project, **Amy Patton** for keeping track of the minutia, **Alice Martina Smith** for going the extra mile in extending assistance during the development of this book, and all the other wonderful support staff at Sams.

Dedication

Pam and Keith dedicate this book to "our families and friends, whose encouragement and support is vital to us."

Tell Us What You Think!

As the reader of this book, *you* are our most important critic and commentator. We value your opinion and want to know what we're doing right, what we could do better, what areas you'd like to see us publish in, and any other words of wisdom you're willing to pass our way.

You can fax, email, or write me directly to let me know what you did or didn't like about this book—as well as what we can do to make our books stronger.

Please note that I cannot help you with technical problems related to the topic of this book, and that because of the high volume of mail I receive, I might not be able to reply to every message.

When you write, please be sure to include this book's title and authors as well as your name and phone or fax number. I will carefully review your comments and share them with the authors and editors who worked on the book.

Fax: 317-581-4770

Email: office_sams@mcp.com

Mail: Mark Taber
           Associate Publisher
           Sams Publishing
           201 West 103rd Street
           Indianapolis, IN 46290 USA

How to Use This Book

The Complete Visual Reference

Each part of this book is made up of a series of short, instructional tasks designed to help you get the most out of Outlook 2000.

Click: Click the left mouse button once.

Double-click: Click the left mouse button twice in rapid succession.

Right-click: Click the right mouse button once.

Right click & Drag

Click & Drag: Position the mouse pointer over the object, click and hold the left mouse button, drag the object to its new location, and release the mouse button.

Selection: Highlights the area onscreen discussed in the step or task.

Keyboard: Type information or data into the indicated location.

Each task includes a series of easy-to-understand steps designed to guide you through the procedure.

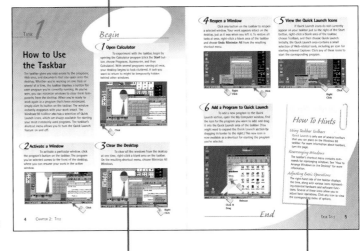

Each step is fully illustrated to show you how it looks onscreen.

Extra hints that tell you how to accomplish a goal are provided in most tasks.

Menus and items you click are shown in **bold**. Words in *italic* are defined in more detail in the glossary. Information you type is in a **special font**.

Continues

If you see this symbol, it means the task you're in continues on the next page.

Introduction

A ccess 2000 is a relational database application. You can use Access to create a database from scratch, or use one of its powerful wizards to guide you through the process of creating a database. The choice is yours.

As you'll discover in this book, database creation doesn't have to be an intimidating task. With some careful up-front planning, you can set up a database that will require very little additional honing, if any, to get it into shape. If you do determine that changes are necessary, though, Access is flexible enough to allow you to make them.

And if you're not comfortable just jumping in and testing the waters, Access includes some sample databases you can play with. (These come complete with sample data, which you'll learn how to replace with your own data in case you want to convert a sample and keep it for your personal use.) We'll show you how to take those sample databases for a test drive and become more familiar with how they're set up and how they work. This will speed up the process of understanding Access 2000's power.

The power of a successful database lies in the information it holds and your ability to sort and retrieve (publish) that data in the manner that best fits your needs. This book walks you through the steps necessary to reach that goal.

Before we begin, some understanding of the terms and naming conventions associated with an Access database will help. (Don't be intimidated. There won't be a quiz! Plus, we'll give you hints and reminders about this stuff throughout the book.)

An Access database consists of elements known as *objects*, which can be any of the following:

✓ **Tables:** As described in Part 4, a *table* is a spreadsheet-style document and is known as a *datasheet* in Access. Each table consists of *fields* (columns) of data, and a collection of fields (a row) makes up a *record*.

✓ **Queries:** As you'll learn in Part 5, a *query* is the way you ask Access questions about your database or alter the information in the database.

✓ **Forms**: In Part 6, you'll learn how to create and use fill-in-the-blank-style forms to view and edit your data.

✓ **Pages**: Access lets you export the data in a table, query, form, or report to a Hypertext Markup Language (HTML) file (page) so that it can be viewed in Internet Explorer and other Web browsers. You'll learn how to do this in Part 8.

✓ **Reports**: In Part 7, you'll learn how to use reports to summarize and print your data.

✓ **Macros**: You can use a macro to perform one or more database actions automatically. (Macros are beyond the scope of this book. For more information on macros, read *Using Microsoft Access 2000*, published by Que Corporation.)

✓ **Modules**: A *module* is a program written in Visual Basic (VB), the programming language included with Access 2000. It's used to automate database functions. (Modules are also beyond the scope of this book. For more information on modules, see *Using Microsoft Access 2000*.)

✓ **Filenames:** The filename (such as addrbook.mdb) you give your database can differ from the name you use to actually title the database (such as Address Book). In this book, we work primarily with one file type (Microsoft Access database files) saved with a specific filename extension (.mdb).

In this book, you'll also notice that we occasionally break one of the rules about naming tables (as in the videos database you'll create in Project 4). For everyday home use, you may prefer to keep your database simple—using field titles you can easily remember or that are, for you, more self-explanatory. For example, you'll create fields with the titles **Male Star** and **Female Star**; if you use the Access wizard to create a videos database, the program suggests that you use **ActorID** and **ActressID** for those field titles. Create databases for your personal use in the way that works easiest for you.

However, if you plan to share the objects in your database with others (even with people who don't necessarily use Access), you may want to use the Leszynski/Reddick naming convention when you choose names for your objects. This convention has certain set rules. For example, you begin the object name with letters that identify it with the object, such as **tbl**, **frm**, **rpt**, **qry**, **mcr**, or **bas**. Object titles using this convention do not have spaces in the titles. For example, you would use a name such as **tblProdInventory** for a Product Inventory table.

By the time you've worked your way through this book, you'll have created several fully functioning databases for your own use. But don't let the word "worked" intimidate you. Read the book, study the sample databases, and do the projects at your own pace and in whatever order is comfortable for you. There's no right or wrong way to read this book—unless you set it aside and don't read it at all.

We wrote *How to Use Microsoft Access 2000* so that you can look at the illustrations and see the process before you begin, if that's your style. Or you can follow along as you do each step, comparing what you see on your screen with what is on the page. You can check the table of contents to find the task that covers what you want to learn or have questions about. We also provide an index to help you find what you're looking for even faster.

This book takes a no-nonsense approach to teaching you how to perform a task. The illustrated step-by-step instructions show you the way and add to your learning experience.

Task

Getting Started with Access 2000

*T*he hardest part of learning any new software program is getting started. Microsoft Access 2000 is no different. It can be pretty intimidating if you don't first master the simple things. Take the time now to learn the basics, and you'll give yourself a solid foundation on which to add the more complicated functions this software offers.

In Part 1, you'll learn how to open and exit the program, how to navigate the Access window, how to use the Access toolbars, how to change Access options, and how to work with Access dialog boxes. ●

How to Open and Exit Access

Before beginning work on any databases, and even before taking a peek at the program, you should familiarize yourself with opening and closing Access 2000.

Begin

1 Open the Start Menu

Choose the **Start** button to open the **Start menu**. From the **Programs** pop-up menu, choose **Microsoft Access**.

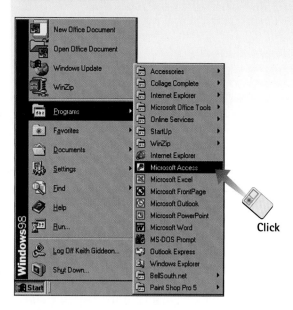

Click

2 Use the Access Startup Dialog Box

Each time you open Access, you will see the **Startup** dialog box. This dialog box allows you to create a new **Blank Access database**, with or without a wizard, or to open an existing Access database so that you can quickly get to work.

3 Open a New Blank Database

For now, select the **Blank Access database** option in the **Create a new database using** area of the **Startup** dialog box.

4 File the New Database

In the **File New Database** dialog box that appears, select a filename (the default **db1.mdb** is fine for now) and click **Create** to open a new **Database** window.

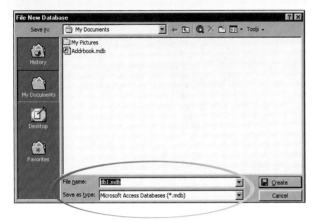

5 Examine the Access Window

You'll immediately notice that the Access window looks similar to other Windows programs you use.

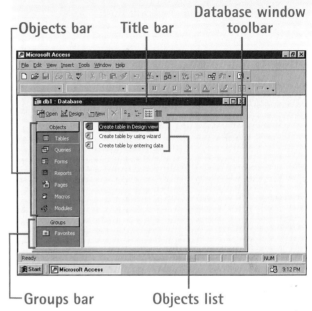

Objects bar   Title bar   Database window toolbar

Groups bar   Objects list

6 Close Access

Closing Access is as simple as closing other Windows programs. Simply click the **Close box** in the upper-right corner of the Access window. Alternatively, you can choose **File, Exit** from the **menu bar**. You may be asked whether you want to save changes to your database, if you have not done so.

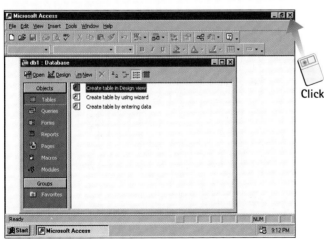

Click

How-To Hints

Create a Desktop Shortcut

To place a shortcut on your desktop for Access, open Windows Explorer and **Find** the file named Msaccess.exe in your \Microsoft Office\Office folder. Drag this file to your desktop. If you want to rename the shortcut, simply right-click the icon and choose **Rename** from the shortcut menu. Type a new name and press the **Enter** key.

End

How to Navigate the Access Window

Although the Access window looks similar to windows in other Windows programs, there are some differences. Gaining an understanding of these differences will help you master Access more quickly. This task is an overview of the Access window. You will learn more in-depth information later in the book. We will be using the **Address Sample Database**, available from the **Startup** dialog box, as an example for this task.

2 Database Toolbar with a Twist

The **Database** toolbar (called the Standard toolbar in other Windows programs) allows you to open files, save and print them, and cut, copy, and paste between them as well. Buttons include **Office Links** to interact with other Office programs, **Analyze** to help you keep your database working smoothly, and **Relationships** to view how your tables interact with each other.

Office Links   Analyze   Relationships

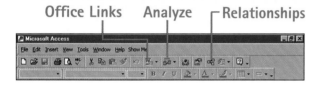

Begin

1 View the Access Window

Start Access as directed in Task 1. From the **Startup** dialog box, select the **Open an existing file** button and then choose **Address Sample Database**. With this database open, you have in front of you all the tools necessary to build or modify the database.

3 The Formatting Toolbar

You select your font styles, sizes, and colors from the **Formatting** toolbar. To display this toolbar, choose **View, Toolbars, Customize**, and then select the **Toolbars** tab and click the box next to **Formatting (Datasheet)**. You can use this toolbar to specify whether gridlines appear in your Access tables. You can also choose special effects for your tables.

Formatting (Datasheet) toolbar   Gridline   Special Effects

4 The Database Window Toolbar

The Database window toolbar allows you to manage your database objects quickly by opening or creating a new object. Choose **Design** to make changes to an object's properties. You can also choose how object icons and object information are viewed in the **Database** window.

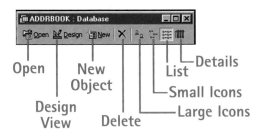

Open
Design View
New Object
Delete
List
Small Icons
Large Icons
Details

5 The Objects Bar

You can use the **Objects bar** to view your options for each of the objects listed. Click a button on the **Objects bar** to see on the right side of the **Database** window a list of files related to that object in your database. You can also choose to create new objects at the top of the **Objects list**.

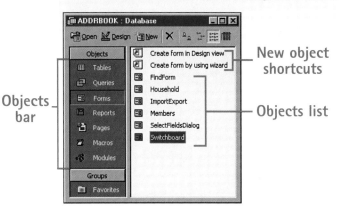

Objects bar
New object shortcuts
Objects list

6 The Status Bar

Keep an eye on the **Status bar** at the bottom of the screen. It will let you know what's going on at all times. Be sure to make a habit of looking at it frequently.

Status bar

End

How to Navigate Access Menus

Access 2000 menus, like the menus in all other Microsoft Office 2000 applications, have undergone a dramatic change since the last version of Office. Microsoft Office 2000 introduces *personalized menus.*

Menus in Access now change as you work. In other words, they're *adaptive* and change according to your work habits. An item on a menu that you use infrequently will not appear when you click to open that menu. Instead, you have to take steps to view all items on it.

Begin

1 Open a Menu

Click **Tools** on the menu bar. The double arrows at the bottom of the menu indicate that you have other choices on this menu.

2 Expand a Menu

To expand an Access menu so that you can view all the items available, you have three choices: Wait a few seconds for the menu to expand, click the arrows at the bottom of the menu, or double-click the menu item on the menu bar to expand the menu immediately.

Double-click

3 Personalized Submenus

Menu personalization also applies to Access submenus. Use them in the same way as a main menu. For example, choose **Tools, Database Utilities** to see a personalized submenu.

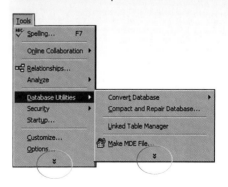

4 View a Shortcut Menu

By right-clicking a toolbar, right-clicking the Database window, or right-clicking in any field in an object window, you can open a **shortcut menu**. Shortcut menus give you quick access to commonly used commands for the object you've clicked.

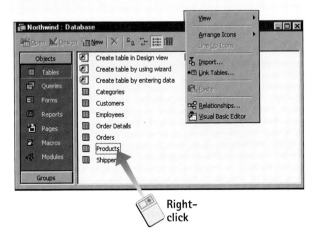

Right-click

6 Set Menu Animations

You can animate your menus by clicking the pull-down menu next to **Menu animations** in the **Customize** dialog box. Your choices are **Slide**, **Unfold**, or **Random** (a combination of **Slide** and **Unfold**).

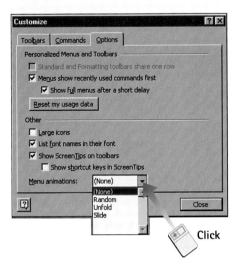

Click

End

5 Customize Access Menus

Access provides options for turning off personalized menus and delaying the speed of menus. From the **View** menu, choose **Toolbars, Customize** to open the **Customize** dialog box. Select the **Options** tab. Under **Personalized Menus and Toolbars**, you can deselect the **Menus show recently used commands first** option to turn off personalized menus, and you can deselect the **Show full menus after a short delay** option to delay the display of full menus.

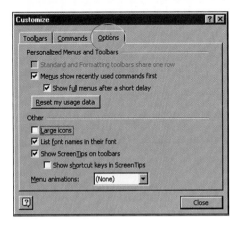

How-To Hints

Turn Off Personalized Menus

If personalized menus are annoying to you, it's easy to turn them off. From the **View** menu, choose **Toolbars, Customize**. On the **Options** tab, under **Personalized Menus and Toolbars**, deselect the **Menus show recently used commands first** check box.

A Shortcut to the Customize Dialog Box

Another way to open the **Customize** dialog box is by right-clicking over any toolbar and then choosing **Customize** from the toolbar's shortcut menu.

How to Choose and Use Toolbars

Everybody is a creature of habit, in one way or another. As you learn your way around Access 2000, you'll form your own preferences about how you perform your work within the program. Until that time, be adventurous. Experiment with the toolbar options described in this task.

Begin

1 Hide a Toolbar

From the **View** menu, choose **Toolbars**. From the submenu, choose the toolbar name you want to hide. To restore the toolbar to the screen, choose **View**, **Toolbars**, **Customize** and select the toolbar you want to restore.

2 Move a Toolbar

To move a *docked* toolbar (a toolbar located at the top of the window), click the **move handle** (the raised gray line above or to the left of a toolbar) and drag it to the desired location. If the toolbar is *floating* (located at some other place on the screen), click its title bar and drag it.

Click & Drag

3 Add or Remove Buttons

If a toolbar seems cluttered to you or you need to add a button to it, click the arrow at the right end of the toolbar. Choose the button to add or remove from the **Add or Remove Buttons** submenu.

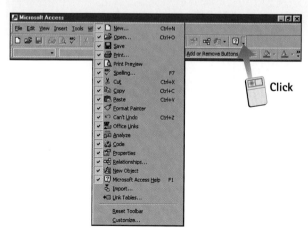

Click

4 Use ScreenTips

If you're not familiar with the purpose of a button, simply point at it with your mouse. In a moment, a **ScreenTip** will pop up to tell you the button's name.

5 Toolbar Options

From the **View** menu, choose **Toolbars, Customize**. Click the **Options** tab in the **Customize** dialog box. Under **Other**, you can choose whether the icons on toolbars are large, whether you see a sample of fonts in the font list box, and whether you want ScreenTips to be activated.

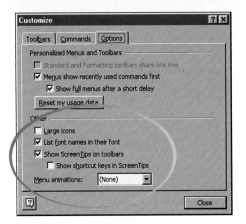

6 Restore Toolbar Defaults

If you have changed a toolbar in any way and want to restore it to its original condition, choose **View, Toolbars, Customize**. On the **Toolbars** tab, choose **Properties**. From the **Selected Toolbar** drop-down menu, select the name of the toolbar and click **Restore Defaults** at the bottom of the **Toolbar Properties** dialog box.

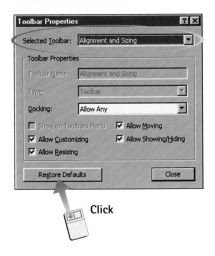

Click

How-To Hints

Finding Additional Toolbars

You can find additional toolbars by choosing **View, Toolbars, Customize**. From the list, select the toolbar you want to activate. To remove a toolbar from the screen, choose **View, Toolbars** and click the toolbar name you want to remove.

End

How to Change Access 2000 Options

By now you may be developing some personal preferences, and you may want to make some changes to how Access behaves for *you*. Fortunately, Access gives you many choices that allow you to customize the program to fit your needs.

Begin

1 Open the Options Dialog Box

Choose **Tools**, **Options**. When the **Options** dialog box opens, take a look at the tab names and familiarize yourself with them.

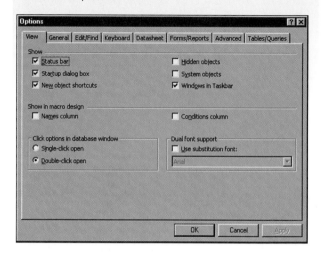

2 Choose What You See

The **View** tab has many options that specify what is included in your Access window. For example, if you don't want the **Startup** dialog box to pop up every time you start Access, click the check box next to that option to deselect it.

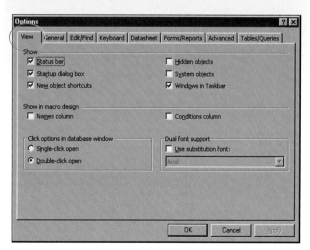

3 Change Print Margins

On the **General** tab, you can change paper margins for the top, bottom, right, and left sides of the pages that you print from Access.

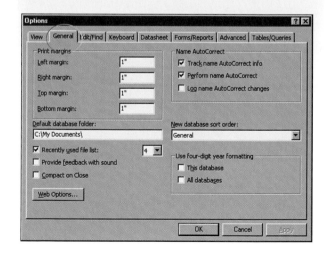

4 Change the Default Folder

If you have another folder in which you want to store your new databases and files, simply change the path listed in the text box under **Default database folder**.

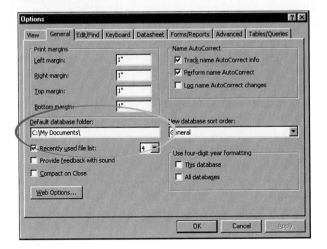

5 Select Confirmation Messages

On the **Edit/Find** tab, click the options under **Confirm** to activate or deactivate warnings or messages before records change, before documents are deleted, or for action queries.

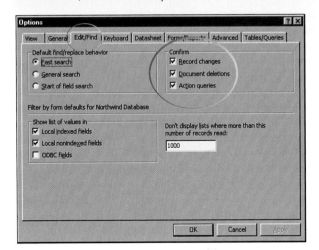

6 Set Default Colors and Fonts

Click the **Datasheet** tab. In the two boxes on the left side of this tab, you can choose your preferences for default colors and fonts.

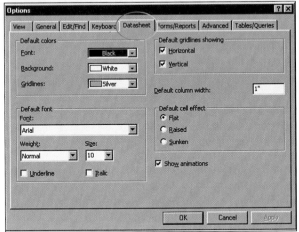

End

How-To Hints

What's This? in Options

To find what other options are for, click the little question mark button in the upper-right corner of the **Options** dialog box. With this button pushed in, click the option for which you want more information.

Task

Finding Help with Access

No matter how adept you are with a software program, you'll need help from time to time. Microsoft Access is loaded with Help options that you can use when you find yourself in a jam.

Among your resources is the ever-present Office Assistant, who *impatiently* waits for you to notice him. Access 2000 also comes with extensive Help files, if you decide to dig into them. Finally, if you have questions that aren't answered in the Help files, Access can launch Internet Explorer to give you even more guidance from the Web.

How to Find Help with the Office Assistant

Clippit and the other Office Assistants are there to offer their help, if and when you want it. Give 'em a chance and they'll entertain you, too—taking some of the humdrum out of your business day. (For example, if you ignore Clippit, he coils into a spring or turns that piece of paper in the background into a makeshift chaise lounge. When you use the Find feature, he rolls the paper into a telescope.) To find out how to make the Office Assistant perform the work you want him to do, read on.

Begin

1 Open the Assistant Balloon

If you need answers and the Office Assistant is showing, press **F1** or click the Assistant. A balloon opens with possible Help topics already listed. If the Assistant isn't showing, choose **Show the Office Assistant** from the **Help** menu.

2 Type a Question

With **Tables** selected in the **Objects bar**, type **How do I change table fonts?** in the balloon text box. Click **Search** or press **Enter**. A list of topics related to your question appears above the text box.

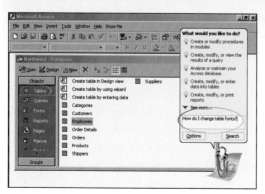

3 Click a Help Topic

If a topic appears that closely resembles the information you need, click that topic. If not, click **See more** for additional topics.

Click

4 Display Messages

For up-to-the-minute help as you work, Office Assistant can display helpful messages from time to time. Click the Assistant and choose **Options**. In the **Office Assistant** dialog box, click the **Guess Help topics** check box to activate these messages.

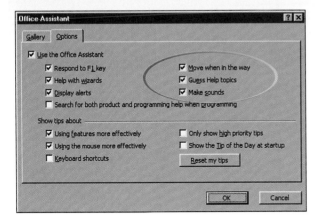

5 Move the Assistant

If the Office Assistant is in your way, you can move him. Click and drag him to the desired location.

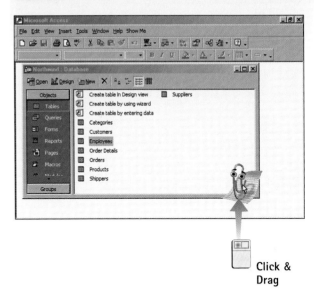

Click & Drag

6 Hide the Assistant

To temporarily remove the Office Assistant from your screen, choose **Hide the Office Assistant** from the **Help** menu. The Office Assistant will reappear when you choose **Help** later.

Click

End

How-To Hints

Office Assistant Shortcut Keys

Here are some helpful keyboard shortcuts for the Office Assistant:

Key	Action
F1	Open the balloon
Esc	Close any Assistant message or tip
Alt+Down arrow	See more Help topics
Alt+Up arrow	See previous Help topics

How to Customize the Office Assistant

Everyone has their own likes and dislikes, and there are several things you can change to make your Office Assistant experience more enjoyable. From changing his appearance to turning him off completely, the choice is yours.

Begin

1 Choose a Different Assistant

Click the Assistant and choose **Options**. In the **Office Assistant** dialog box, click the **Gallery** tab. Click the **Back** and **Next** buttons to scroll through the available Assistants. Click **OK** when you've chosen your new friend. (You may be prompted to have your Access CD-ROM handy.)

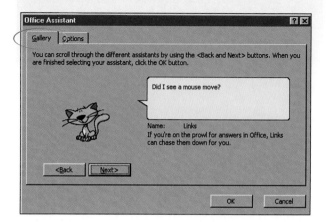

2 Mute the Assistant

To turn off the sound capabilities of the Assistant, click it and choose **Options**. On the **Options** tab of the **Office Assistant** dialog box, click the **Make sounds** check box to deselect this option.

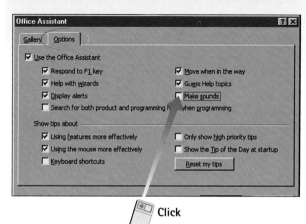

Click

3 Change General Options

The top half of the **Options** tab of the **Office Assistant** dialog box gives you several choices for setting preferences. Click the check box next to each option to select or deselect it. For an explanation of each item, click the **What's This?** button (the question mark) in the upper-right corner of the dialog box and then click the item in question.

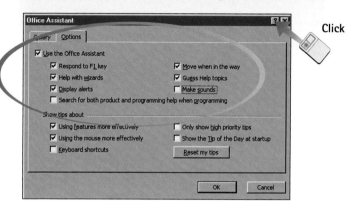

Click

4 Choose Help Tips

Help tips can come in handy, but you may find that you don't need them as often after you've become familiar with Access. In the bottom half of the **Options** tab of the **Office Assistant** dialog box, click the check box for each option you want to change.

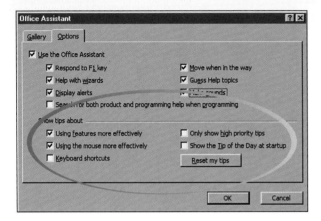

5 Reset Help Tips

If you have selected the **Show the Tip of the Day at startup** option, you may want to see again the tips that have appeared already. On the **Options** tab of the **Office Assistant** dialog box, click **Reset my tips**. The Office Assistant shows you that this has been accomplished.

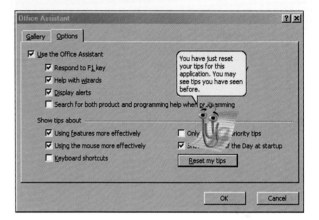

6 Turn the Assistant Off

Some people get annoyed by the Assistant. If you feel the need to turn him off, simply click him and choose **Options**. In the **Options** tab, click the check box for **Use the Office Assistant** to deselect it. All the options in the dialog box will be grayed out. The Assistant will not return until you choose **Show the Office Assistant** from the **Help** menu.

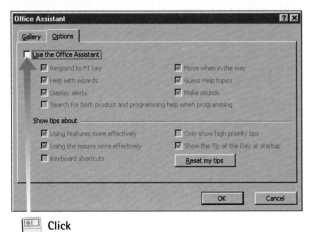

⌨ Click

How-To Hints

Why Isn't My New Assistant Available?

When you install Access 2000, some features are left out of the installation to save disk space. At times, while using Access, you will be asked to insert your Access or Office 2000 CD-ROM so that the program can find the features you're trying to use. Keeping your Access 2000 CD-ROM handy can save you time as you work in Access.

What Is the Show Me Menu?

The sample databases in Access have an extra menu item called **Show Me**. From this menu, you can find special help-related information on that particular sample database.

End

How to Use the Office Help System

Even if you have the Office Assistant turned off, you still have access to an abundance of help. You can use the Access 2000 Help files to view subjects formatted like a table of contents, ask questions of an answer wizard, search an index of keywords, and print help topics.

Begin

1 Open Access Help

With the Office Assistant disabled (see the last step in Task 2), choose **Microsoft Access Help** from the **Help** menu.

Click

2 Ask the Answer Wizard

Click the **Answer Wizard** tab. Type a question into the **What would you like to do?** box, and then click **Search** or press **Enter**. A list of topics appears in the **Select topic to display** pane. Click a topic and read the information in the right pane.

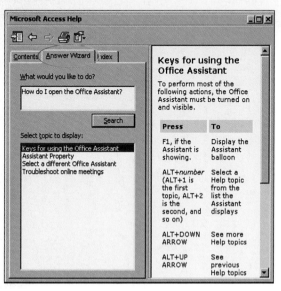

3 View Help by Content

Click the **Contents** tab of the **Help** dialog box. Click the + next to **Creating and Working with Databases** to expand that topic's contents. When you find a topic you want more information on, click it (in this case, it's **Create a database**). View the information in the right pane, and select a topic by clicking it under **What do you want to do?**

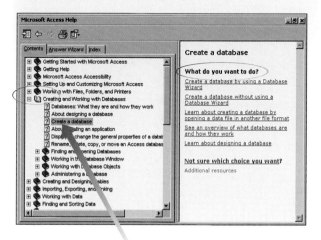

Click

4 Search the Index

Click the **Index** tab and type a keyword (or words) in the **Type keywords** text box. Click **Search** or press **Enter**. A list of related topics appears under **Choose a topic**. If you find a relevant topic, click it and view the information in the right pane.

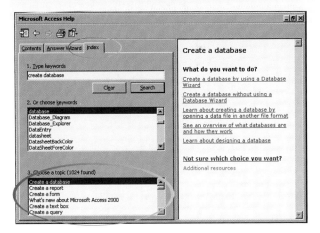

5 Print a Topic

When a Help topic is listed in the right pane, you can print it by clicking the **Print** button on the **Access Help** toolbar. If you're in the **Contents** tab, Access asks whether you want to print the selected topic or all topics within the currently selected heading.

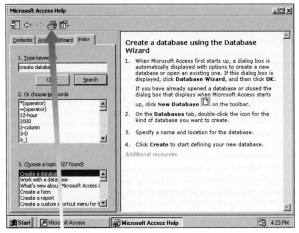

 Click

6 Print All Heading Topics

If you want to print all topics within a heading, select a topic on the **Contents** tab and click the **Print** button in the **Access Help** toolbar. The **Print Topics** dialog box opens. Click the button next to **Print the selected heading and all subtopics**, and then click **OK**.

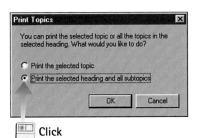

Click

End

How-To Hints

More About the Microsoft Access Help Box

The five buttons above the **Help** tabs in the Help dialog box can be quite useful. From left to right, the first is the **Hide Tabs** button; it hides the tabbed pane. Next is the **Back** button; click it to go one topic back in the topic pane. The function of the **Forward** button is opposite that of the **Back** button. The **Print** button is obvious. The **Options** button gives you a menu list of options, including some of the same functions as the buttons to the left of it.

How to Find Help on the Web

For those times when you want more information than is contained in the Access Help files, you can go online to get answers on the Web (assuming that you have a way to connect to the Internet). Access 2000 even makes connecting to **Office on the Web** easy. If you're not already online when you perform the following steps, you'll see your **Dial Up Connection** box so that you can connect and search for the answers you need.

Begin

1 Go to Office on the Web

From the **Help** menu, choose **Office on the Web**, which takes you to an Access Welcome Web page on the Microsoft Web site. It's best to use Internet Explorer for these next steps; unless you have another browser set as your default, Internet Explorer opens automatically when you perform this step.

Click

2 Click the Assistance Link

In the navigation area on the left side of the Web page, click the **Assistance** link.

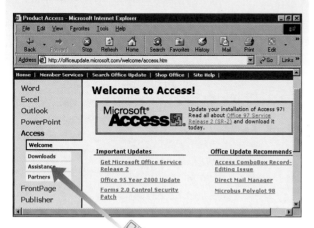

Click

3 Use the Knowledge Base

If you want to access a huge collection of articles on Access, written by Microsoft, click the **Knowledge Base Articles about Access** link under the **Microsoft Technical Support** heading on the Access Assistance Web page. Be forewarned: This material can get quite *techy*.

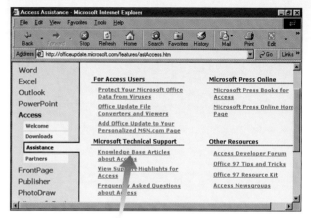

 Click

4 View Support Highlights

If you need information about Access security, add-ins, service packs, and hot issues related to Access, click the **View Support Highlights for Access** link on the Access Assistance Web page.

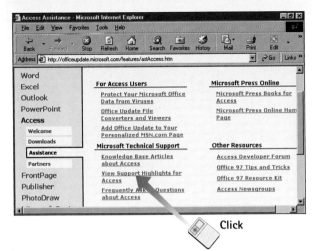

Click

5 Read Access FAQs

Many people ask Microsoft the same questions concerning a topic. To take a peek at a list of these Frequently Asked Questions (FAQs), click the **Frequently Asked Questions about Access** link on the Access Assistance Web page.

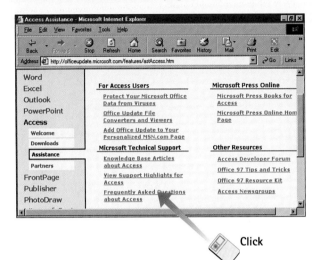

Click

6 Choose Other Resources

Under the **Other Resources** heading of the Access Assistance Web page, you can find valuable information about Access tips and tricks, the Office Resource Kit, and Access newsgroups. Click the link for which you want more information.

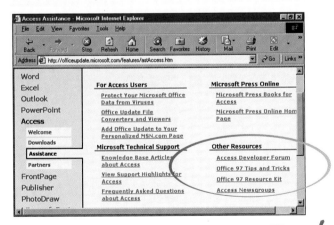

End

How-To Hints

There's More Than One Way to Skim a Stat

Deciding whether or not you want to use the Office Assistant is a matter of personal choice.

Pam loves the Office Assistant; Keith doesn't. If you agree with Keith, follow the directions in Task 2, Step 6 to turn off the Office Assistant completely.

If you prefer to find Help as answers to questions you formulate yourself, type your questions in the Office Assistant text box or use the text box on the Help **Answer Wizard** tab.

Also, you can find Knowledge Base articles, technical support, and FAQs by using Office on the Web Access Assistance.

Project 1

Northwind Sample Database Tutorial

There's a reason artists imitate the masters early in their careers. They want to learn from those who had been around the palette and knew what they were doing. The same motive is why this first project introduces you to the **Northwind Traders** sample database that comes with Access 2000. You can manipulate this database to your heart's content. As you study the examples and make experimental changes to this sample database, you'll get some ideas about how best to plan your own database designs.

1 Open Access

To start Access, open the **Start** menu and choose **Programs, Microsoft Access**. (In some cases, Access may reside in an Office 2000 folder on the Start menu.)

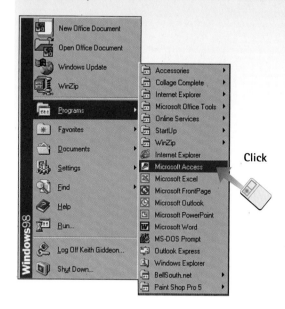

Click

2 Select Northwind

Access opens a dialog box that gives you the choices **Blank Access database**, **Access database wizards, pages, and projects**, and **Open an existing file**. The latter is selected by default. Scroll down the list that appears in that window and click **Northwind Sample Database**. Click **OK**.

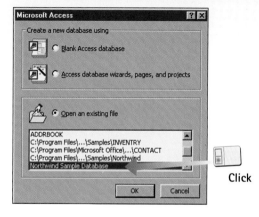

Click

3 The Northwind Startup Screen

Access displays a "Welcome to Northwind Traders" introduction screen. Click the **Don't show this screen again** box if you don't want to see this screen the next time you open this file. Click **OK**.

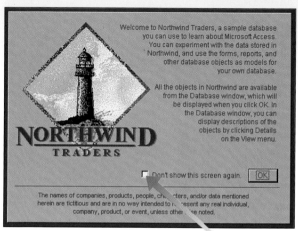

Click

4 Open the Main Switchboard Form

From the **Northwind Database** window that appears, open the Main Switchboard form: In the Objects bar, click the **Forms** button. From the Objects list in the right pane, select **Main Switchboard** and then click **Open**. You use the Main Switchboard form to control navigation in your Access database or project (see Task 5 in Part 3, "Creating and Working with Database Files").

Click

5 The Main Switchboard Form

Access automatically creates a **Main Switchboard** form each time you use a Wizard to create a database. Its purpose is to help you move around the database.

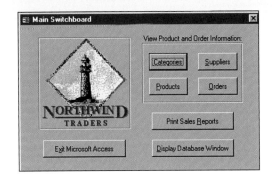

6 Get Help

To get Help with the Northwind database, click the **Office Assistant** or open the **Help** menu. Northwind also has a **Show Me** menu option you can click for help with the area on which you're currently working. Refer to Part 2, "Finding Help with Access," for more information.

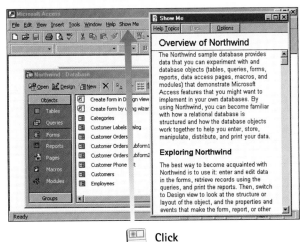

Click

7 Pick a Table in Northwind

Click the **Northwind: Database** button on the taskbar to bring the Database window to the foreground (moving the Main Switchboard to the background). In the Objects bar, click **Tables**, choose **Suppliers**, and then click **Open**.

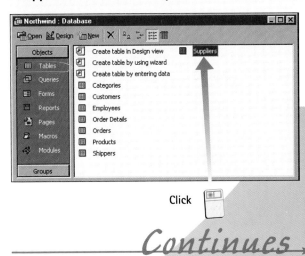

Click

Continues

8 Tables and Facts

Each database table stores details about a class of information or facts. In the **Suppliers: Table** window, notice **Supplier ID**, **Company Name**, **Contact Name**, and other aspects of the **Suppliers** table.

Supplier ID	Company Name	Contact Name
1	Exotic Liquids	Charlotte Cooper
2	New Orleans Cajun Delights	Shelley Burke
3	Grandma Kelly's Homestead	Regina Murphy
4	Tokyo Traders	Yoshi Nagase
5	Cooperativa de Quesos 'Las Cabras'	Antonio del Valle Saavedra
6	Mayumi's	Mayumi Ohno
7	Pavlova, Ltd.	Ian Devling
8	Specialty Biscuits, Ltd.	Peter Wilson
9	PB Knäckebröd AB	Lars Peterson
10	Refrescos Americanas LTDA	Carlos Diaz
11	Heli Süßwaren GmbH & Co. KG	Petra Winkler
12	Plutzer Lebensmittelgroßmärkte AG	Martin Bein

Record: 1 of 29

9 Select a Field

Each fact in a database table is stored in a *field*. Move the mouse pointer above the **Contact Name** field heading until it becomes a down arrow, and then click the heading to select that field. Move the mouse and click anywhere on the screen to de-select the field.

Supplier ID	Company Name	Contact Name
1	Exotic Liquids	Charlotte Cooper
2	New Orleans Cajun Delights	Shelley Burke
3	Grandma Kelly's Homestead	Regina Murphy
4	Tokyo Traders	Yoshi Nagase
5	Cooperativa de Quesos 'Las Cabras'	Antonio del Valle Saavedra
6	Mayumi's	Mayumi Ohno
7	Pavlova, Ltd.	Ian Devling
8	Specialty Biscuits, Ltd.	Peter Wilson
9	PB Knäckebröd AB	Lars Peterson
10	Refrescos Americanas LTDA	Carlos Diaz
11	Heli Süßwaren GmbH & Co. KG	Petra Winkler
12	Plutzer Lebensmittelgroßmärkte AG	Martin Bein

Record: 1 of 29

 Click

10 Data Types in Design View

Each field has a data type that varies based on the kind of data the field stores. You must be in Design view if you want to modify or set the data type for a given field. Click the **Design View** button in the toolbar to change to Design view.

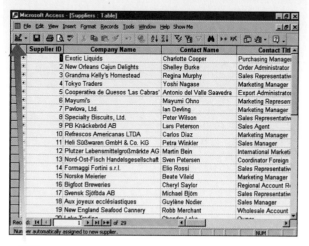

 Click

How-To Hints

About Data Types

Data types include **Text** (up to 255 characters), **Memo** (lengthy text of up to 65,535 characters), **Number**, **Date/Time**, **Currency**, **AutoNumber** (for automatic sequential records), **Yes/No**, **OLE Object** (up to 1 gigabyte, limited by disk space), **Hyperlink**, and **Lookup Wizard** (used to choose a value from another table or list). (Note that there are instances where the size of the Memo field may be limited by the database size.)

11 View Suppliers Data Type Field

To look at the data types for each field in the **Suppliers** database, click each field. The appropriate information appears in the **Field Properties** area in the bottom half of the window. Click the **Lookup** tab to see **Display Control** information.

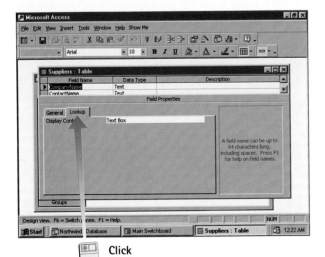

Click

12 Look at the Employees Table

Each set of facts in a table row equals one *record*. Display the **Database** window again. In the Objects bar, choose **Tables**. From the Objects list, choose **Employees** and click **Open**. Notice that there are nine employee records in the **Employees** database.

		Employee ID	Last Name	First Name	Title	Title Of	Birth Da
▶	+	1	Davolio	Nancy	Sales Representative	Ms.	08-Dec-1
	+	2	Fuller	Andrew	Vice President, Sales	Dr.	19-Feb-1
	+	3	Leverling	Janet	Sales Representative	Ms.	30-Aug-1
	+	4	Peacock	Margaret	Sales Representative	Mrs.	19-Sep-1
	+	5	Buchanan	Steven	Sales Manager	Mr.	04-Mar-1
	+	6	Suyama	Michael	Sales Representative	Mr.	02-Jul-1
	+	7	King	Robert	Sales Representative	Mr.	29-May-1
	+	8	Callahan	Laura	Inside Sales Coordinator	Ms.	09-Jan-1
	+	9	Dodsworth	Anne	Sales Representative	Ms.	02-Jul-1
*		(AutoNumber)					

Record: 1 of 9

13 Use the Supplier Drop-Down List

Display the **Database** window again. From the Objects list, open the **Products** table. Click an entry in the **Supplier** column to reveal a drop-down list of all suppliers. Such lists simplify data entry when new products are added to the table.

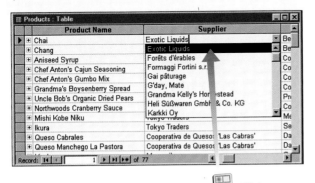

Click

Continues

How-To Hints

The Lookup Tab

When you select a control for a property, any additional properties needed to configure the control are also displayed on the **Lookup** tab (refer to Step 11). When a field doesn't contain a **Display Control**, that area will be blank. In the Northwind **Suppliers** table, all but the **SupplierID** and **HomePage** fields have **Text** as their **Display Control**.

14 Show Table Relationships

From the **Tools** menu, select **Relationships** to see an overview of all the tables in the Northwind database. The connecting lines indicate the relationships between the tables.

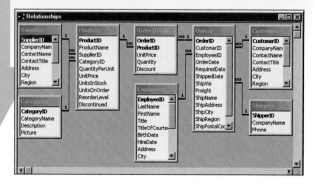

15 Use Quintessential Quality Queries

You don't get too many chances to use a "q" word in everyday conversation. However, when it comes to the work you do in Access, you'll use *queries* a lot. Display the **Database** window again. From the Objects bar, choose **Queries**.

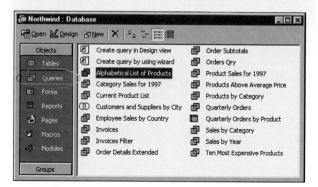

16 View the Current Product List Query

From the Objects list in the **Database** window, click **Current Product List** and then click **Open**. The **Current Product List** query shows entries from the **Product List** table only if each entry has not been discontinued (that is, if each entry is current).

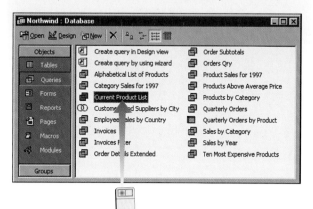

Click

17 Limit Records Returned in a Query

A query can use criteria, or properties, to gather or limit the data displayed from two or more related tables. The **Current Product List** query is an example of this type. Click the **Design** button in the **Database** window toolbar to see the structure of the query.

Click

18 Examine the Query Structure

Notice that the word *No* appears in the **Criteria** line for the **Discontinued** field. This tells you that the **Current Product List** query excludes data from the **Product List** table if that data has been marked as discontinued in that table.

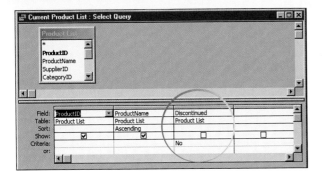

19 View the Product Sales for 1997

In the Objects bar in the **Database** window, select **Queries**, choose **Product Sales for 1997** from the Objects list, and click **Open**. This query shows information about the 286 items sold in 1997 by **Category Name**, **Product Name**, **Product Sales**, and **ShippedQuarter**.

Category Name	Product Name	Product Sales	ShippedQuarter
Beverages	Chai	$705.60	Qtr 1
Beverages	Chai	$878.40	Qtr 2
Beverages	Chai	$1,174.50	Qtr 3
Beverages	Chai	$2,128.50	Qtr 4
Beverages	Chang	$2,720.80	Qtr 1
Beverages	Chang	$228.00	Qtr 2
Beverages	Chang	$2,061.50	Qtr 3
Beverages	Chang	$2,028.25	Qtr 4
Beverages	Chartreuse verte	$590.40	Qtr 1
Beverages	Chartreuse verte	$360.00	Qtr 2
Beverages	Chartreuse verte	$1,100.70	Qtr 3
Beverages	Chartreuse verte	$2,424.60	Qtr 4
Beverages	Côte de Blaye	$25,127.36	Qtr 1

Record: 1 of 286

20 Set Criteria for a Query

Keeping the **Product Sales for 1997** query open, click the **Design** button in the **Database** window toolbar. Note the criteria under **ShippedDate**. As you will learn in Task 6 of Part 5, "Working with Database Table Queries," you can set criteria so that they don't change, so that they prompt for information, or so that values are set from a custom dialog box or by using an SQL SELECT statement.

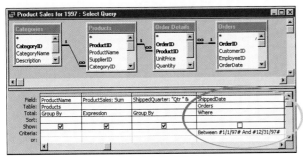

Continues

How-To Hints

What's a Query?

A **query** is the statement you give Access (either by writing it yourself or by using a wizard to create it). The query tells Access what kind of information (from one or more tables) you want to retrieve, sort, or manipulate in some way. For more information on queries, see Part 5. You may also want to refer to *Sams Teach Yourself Microsoft Access in 21 Days* (published by Sams).

21 Category Sales for 1997

Sometimes one query uses the result from another query to calculate its total, such as in the case of the **Category Sales for 1997** query, which uses the results from the **Product Sales for 1997** query.

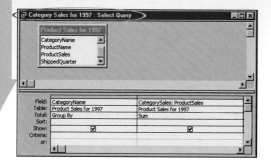

22 View a Union Query in SQL View

From the **Northwind Database** window (with **Queries** selected in the Objects bar), choose **Customers and Suppliers by City** and then click **Open** to display a union query. Union and crosstab queries merge data from several tables.

23 Open the Phone List Form

In the **Objects** bar of the **Database** window, click **Forms** to display the names of those forms available in the Northwind sample database. From the Objects list in the right pane, choose the **Customer Phone List** and click **Open**.

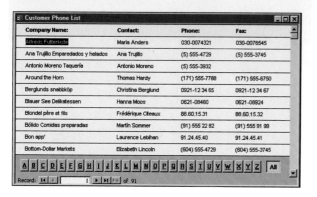

24 Get a Good-Looking Printout

The forms in Northwind are designed to look good; the printouts are attractive, too. To see what the **Customer Phone List** printout would look like, if you printed it, choose **File**, **Print Preview**. The **Print Preview** window opens.

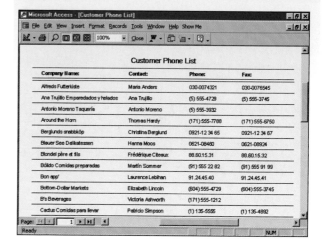

25 Present Data with Reports

Study the reports in Northwind for inspiration on ways you can calculate totals and group, sort, and arrange data. To see the reports, choose **Reports** from the Objects bar in the **Database** window.

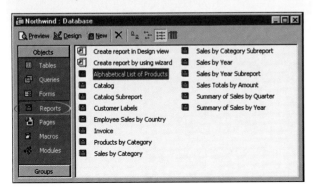

26 Ready Data for the Internet

You can use data access pages (click the **Pages** button on the Objects bar in the **Database** window) to enter, edit, and manipulate data to get it ready to publish to an intranet or to the Internet.

End

How-To Hints

Use Northwind to Experiment

Northwind lets you see a fully functioning database design, so take advantage of that. Use the fields in Northwind to see what data types you'll need to use in your own database design.

Elsewhere in This Book

As you work your way through the other projects in this book, you'll explore in a bit more depth much of the information we touched on in this project. In those later projects, we'll also explain some of the ways you can customize and modify your database. You can read more about tables in Part 4, about queries in Part 5, and about forms in Part 6. In Part 7, you learn how to obtain great-looking printouts of your data.

Other Things to Read

After you explore this book, you'll probably find yourself bitten by the database bug and want to know more. Let us recommend *Sams Teach Yourself Microsoft Access in 21 Days* (published by Sams) and *Using Microsoft Access* (published by Que Corporation).

Task

Creating and Working with Database Files

An understanding of Access basics is essential to understanding the program and using it effectively. These skills make up the cornerstone of your Access experience.

An Access database is actually a *collection of files*. This collection includes numerous tables, forms, reports, queries, and macros, each of which is a separate file. Each file—whether it is a table, a form, or some other type of object—contains data useful to the other objects in the database. For example, a query uses data from tables, and tables use data from forms.

In this part, you learn how to create and open database files and how to save disk space by compacting these files. In addition, you learn how to protect your databases by securing them with a password and backing them up in case of problems. ●

How to Open an Access Database

Opening a database is, of course, the first thing you do when you begin to work in Access. There's more than one way to do this, and you'll see them all in this task.

Begin

1 Open from the Startup Dialog Box

When you open Access, you'll see the **Startup** dialog box (unless you've disabled it in Options). With the **Open an existing file** option selected, double-click a file in the file list.

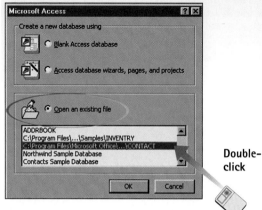

Double-click

2 Click the Open Button

A second way to open a database is to click the **Open** button on the **Database** toolbar. This brings up the **Open** dialog box.

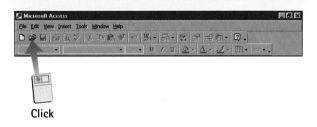

Click

3 Choose the Database

In the **Open** dialog box, double-click the filename of the database you want to open.

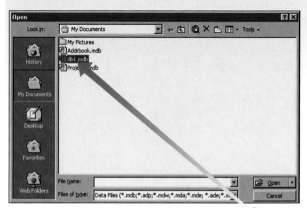

Double-click

4 Open from the Menu Bar

To open a database from the menu bar, choose **File, Open**. The **Open** dialog box appears.

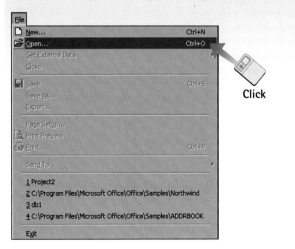

Click

5 Choose the Database

Just as in Step 3, double-click the filename of the database you want to open from the **Open** dialog box.

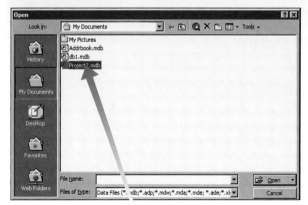

Double-click

6 Open from Recently Used List

If you've recently worked on a database, you can probably open it from the recently used list in the **File** menu. Simply click the file you want to open if it appears on the list.

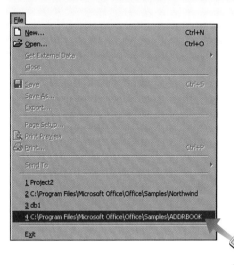

Click

End

How-To Hints

Customize the Recently Used File List

To change the number of files seen on the recently used file list, choose **Tools, Options**. On the **General** tab, make your selection from the pull-down menu to the right of the Recently used file list option.

How to Search for Files in Access

If you have many databases, you may find it difficult to locate a file you haven't worked on in a while. Fortunately, Access has a search tool that can help you find files more efficiently.

With Access 2000, you can save particular searches for future use and search for files by their file properties.

Begin

1 Prepare a Search

From the **File** menu, choose **Open**. Or, click the **Open** button on the **Database** toolbar to view the **Open** dialog box.

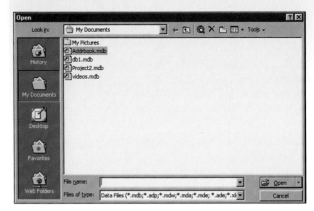

2 Open the Find Dialog Box

Choose **Tools, Find** on the toolbar to open the **Find** dialog box.

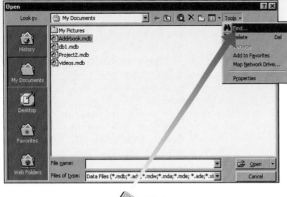

 Click

3 Select the Search Folder

Select the drive or folder you want to search from the **Look in** box near the bottom of the dialog box. Use the down arrow to browse your drive(s).

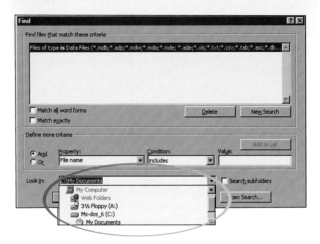

4 Choose the Search Property

Because you're searching for filenames, make sure that **File name** is selected in the **Property** box.

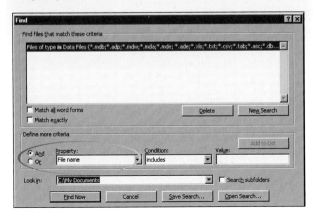

5 Choose the Condition

Choose a condition based on your value. It's best to keep this option set to **includes** because this option provides the widest search.

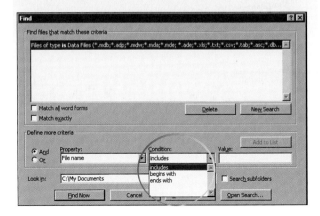

6 Type a Value

In the **Value** box, type the word or phrase for which you want to search. In this example, you're searching for a database with the word *Billing* in its filename.

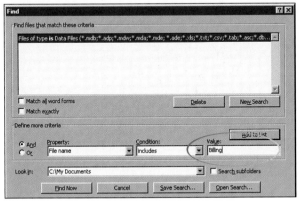

How-To Hints

Search More Than One Drive at a Time

You can search more than one drive at a time by typing each drive name in the **Look in** text box, separating them with semicolons. For example: `C:\;D:\;E:\`.

What You Can't Search For

You cannot use the Find feature to look for files by searching for text within an Access database or within an Access project file.

Continues →

7 Choose Add to List

Click the **Add to List** button. This action places the value you typed (in this example, *Billing*) into the **Find files that match these criteria** box.

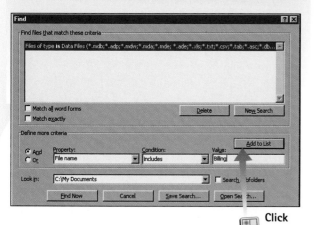

Click

8 Start the Search

Click the **Find Now** button. Access begins searching for files based on the options you've chosen. Any matching files are shown in the **Open** dialog box.

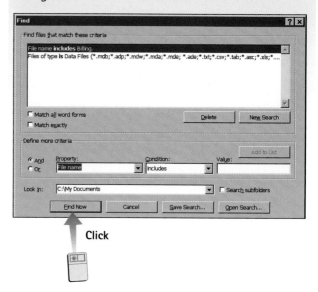

Click

9 Use File Properties

You can also search for files in Access by using other file properties, such as comments, company name, and date created. Follow Steps 1 through 3 to select the folders or drives you want to search, and then continue with Step 10.

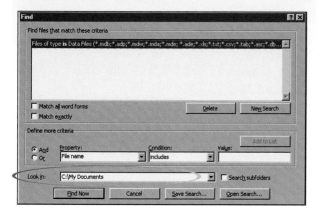

10 Select the Search Property

In the **Property** box, select the type of file property you want to search for. You can select author, creation date, comments, or anything else usually listed with a file's properties. Type a word, phrase, or date in the **Value** box and click **Add to List**.

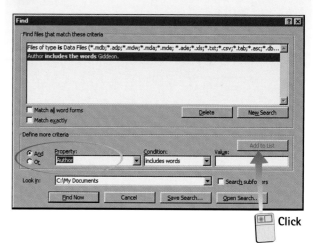

Click

11 Save a Search

If you want to save the search criteria you have entered for later use, click **Save Search** at the bottom of the **Find** dialog box. You are prompted for a search name. Type one and click **OK**.

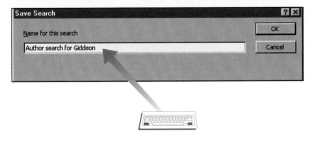

12 Start Properties Search

Click the **Find Now** button to begin searching for files using the specified file properties. (You may be asked to insert your CD-ROM at this point, so have it handy.) Any matching files are displayed in the **Open** dialog box.

End

How-To Hints

More About File Properties

To ensure better search capabilities in the future, be sure to add information to your database's properties. Select **File, Database Properties** and add any relevant information in the spaces provided.

3

How to Create a Database with a Wizard

Creating a database is a simple task with the Database Wizard. Make a few choices and you have a new database. What could be easier?

Begin

1 Open the Wizard

From the **File** menu, choose **New**. Alternatively, select **Access database wizards, pages, and projects** from the **Startup** dialog box and choose **OK**. In the **New** dialog box, click the **Databases** tab and double-click the **Contact Management** icon.

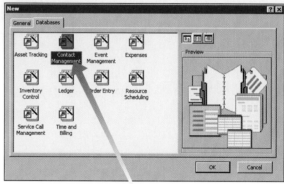

 Double-click

2 Save the Database

In the File **New Database** dialog box, type the filename **Contact Management1** for your new database (we'll use this database again in Task 5) and click **Create**. The first pane of the wizard appears. Click **Next**.

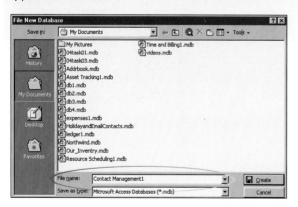

3 Choose Table Fields

The next window allows you to add fields to the tables in the database you are creating. Highlight the table name in the left box and choose the fields you want for that table in the right box. For this example, use the default fields. Click **Next**.

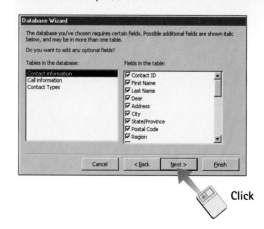

Click

4 Select a Screen Style

The wizard gives you a choice of screen display styles for your forms and reports. Click a style to see a preview in the left pane. Make your final choice and click **Next**.

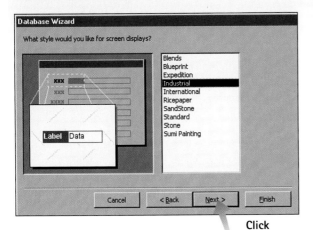

Click

5 Choose a Print Style

Now you have a choice of print styles. Check out the previews to see the available font styles. Make a choice and click **Next**.

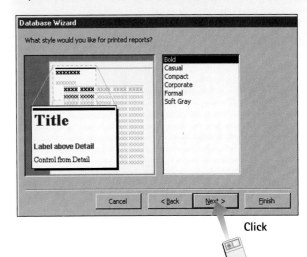

Click

6 Type a Database Title

Type **Contact Management** in the text box provided. This is the title you want the new database to have. Click **Next**.

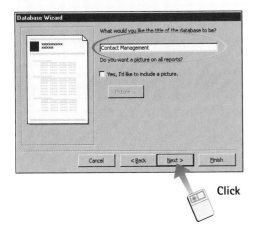

Click

7 Finish the Wizard

Depending on your wishes, click the check boxes next to **Yes, start the database** and **Display Help on using a database** and then click **Finish**. That's it, you have created a database.

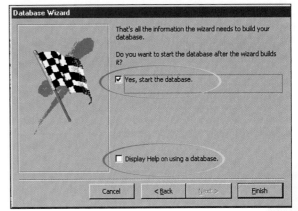

End

How to Use the Switchboard Manager

A **swichboard** is a central location for your database operations. Buttons on the switchboard exist for the most common tasks you perform in the database.

If you have built a database without the aid of the Database Wizard and want to use a switchboard with your database, you can use the Switchboard Manager to add a switchboard. You should have data in your database before building a switchboard.

Begin

1 Open Switchboard Manager

Open a database you created without a wizard and choose **Tools, Database Utilities, Switchboard Manager**. You will see a dialog box asking whether you want to create a switchboard. Click **Yes**.

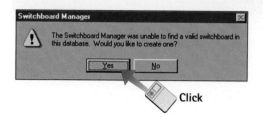

Click

2 Edit the Switchboard

In the **Switchboard Manager** dialog box, click **Edit** to view the **Edit Switchboard Page** dialog box.

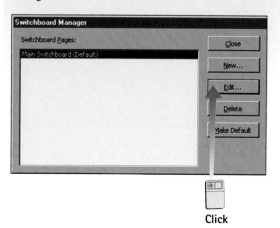

Click

3 Name the Switchboard

Type a name for the switchboard in the **Switchboard Name** text box. (If this is the first switchboard for your database, it's best to leave this name as **Main Switchboard**.) Click **New**.

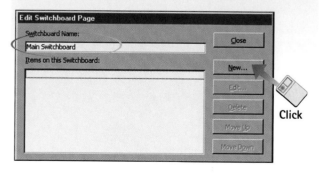

Click

4 Edit a Switchboard Item

In the **Edit Switchboard Item** dialog box, type the name of the first switchboard button in the **Text** box. For example, type **Preview Clients List Report**. The text you type will appear next to a button on the switchboard.

5 Choose an Item Command

Choose a command from the **Command** pull-down menu. In this example, you want to preview a report, so choose **Open Report** from the **Command** pull-down menu.

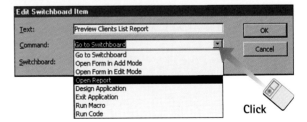

Click

6 Select the Item to Open

The name of the last box in the **Edit Switchboard Item** dialog box changes depending on which command you choose. From this box, select the file you want the command to open. In this example, you want the **Client Listing** report to open.

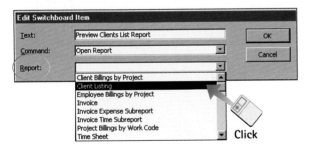

Click

7 Add More Items

To add additional items to your switchboard, repeat Steps 4 through 6.

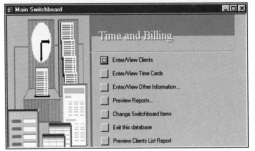

End

How-To Hints

Branch One Switchboard to Another

To link two or more switchboards to each other, create an item for a switchboard using the command **Go To Switchboard**. Then select the name of the switchboard in the box named **Switchboard**.

Make a Switchboard Open with a Database

You can force a switchboard to open automatically with a database by highlighting the name of the switchboard in the **Switchboard Manager** dialog box and clicking **Make Default**.

How to Use the Switchboard to Access Objects

This task shows you how easy it is to access objects using the switchboard. For this task, you'll use a database called **Contact Management1**, which was created using the skills you learned in Task 3.

Begin

1 Open the Database

From the **File** menu, choose **Open**. Alternatively, click the **Open** button on the **Database** toolbar to view the **Open** dialog box. Choose **Contact Management1.mdb** and click **Open**.

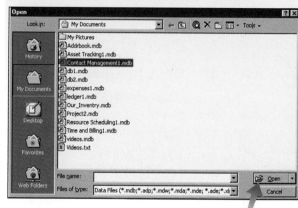

Click

2 Choose a Data Category

On the **Main Switchboard**, click the **Enter/View Contacts** button to open a contacts form.

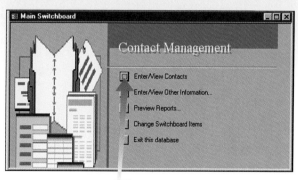

 Click

3 Enter Contact Information

Add information to the appropriate fields. Click the **Page 2** button to see additional fields. Add as little information as you like now; you can always add more later.

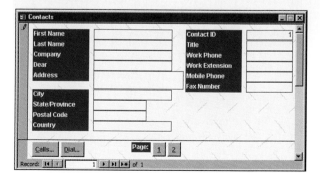

4 Close the Form

When you're done filling in the information for a contact, click the **Close** box in the upper-right corner of the form. Access automatically saves the data.

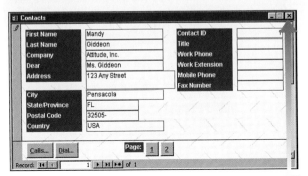

Click

5 Enter Other Information

On the **Main Switchboard**, click **Enter/View Other Information** to open a second switchboard called **Forms Switchboard**. You'll often need more contact types than Access creates for you. If you enter additional contact types into the database, you will be able to select the contact type from the drop-down menu at the bottom of a Contact form. Click **Enter/View Contact Types**.

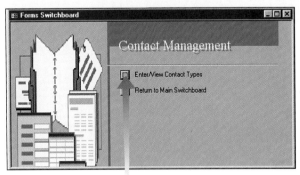

Click

6 Enter a Contact Type

Fill in a contact type. You can choose any type of contact you have, such as friend, business, church, and so on. When you're done, click the **Close** box to go back to the **Forms Switchboard**. Click **Return to Main Switchboard**.

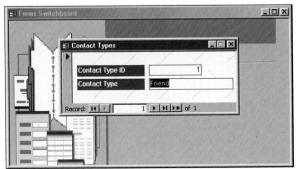

End

How-To Hints

For More Information on Forms

This task showed how to access a data-entry form from a switchboard. For more information on forms, see Part 6, "Creating and Working with Access Forms."

More About Contact Types

In the **Contact Management** database, you can use contact types to categorize your contacts. Contact types are useful when you are trying to create a report or query for a single category of contacts such as "business" or "little league."

How to Use the Database Window

The **Database** window is the main interface to your database objects. It is the window that opens (along with the switchboard, if one is available) when you open a database in Access. By using the Database window, you can open, delete, edit, and rename database objects.

Begin

1 Examine the Database Window

Take a look at the **Database** window and get familiar with the **toolbar**, the **Objects bar**, and the **Objects list**.

Objects bar   Objects list   Toolbar

2 Choose an Object Type

To choose an object type, click a button in the **Objects bar** (**Forms** in the example). The available objects are shown in the **Objects list** in the right pane of the **Database** window.

Click

3 Open an Object

Click an object in the **Objects list** (**Contacts** in the example) and click **Open** from the Database window toolbar. Alternatively, double-click the object.

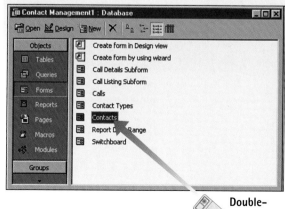

Double-click

4 Create a New Object

To create a new table, form, report, or any other object, select the object type from the **Objects bar** and click **New** on the Database window toolbar. In the **New "Object"** dialog box, select the option for the manner in which you want to create the new object. (We suggest using the wizard.) Click **OK** and follow the instructions to create that object.

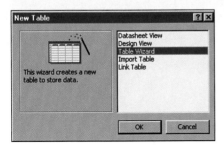

5 Open an Object in Design View

You can open an object in Design view by clicking the object in the **Objects list** and clicking **Design** from the Database window toolbar. You can now edit the object. Click the **Close** box when you are done editing in Design view.

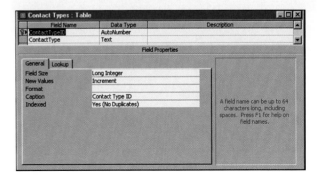

6 Delete an Object

To delete an object, select the object from the **Objects list** and click the **Delete** button on the Database window toolbar. Alternatively, right-click the object in the **Objects list** and select **Delete** from the shortcut menu. A third option is to select the object and then press the **Delete** key on the keyboard.

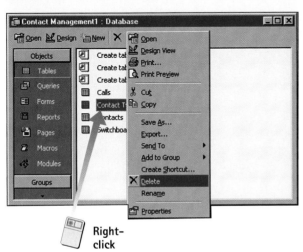

Right-click

7 Rename an Object

To rename an object, right-click the object name in the **Objects list** and choose **Rename** from the shortcut menu. Alternatively, click the object name once, and then click it again. When the black box appears around the object name, type the new name and press **Enter**.

Continues

8 Refresh the Database Window

Make sure that your **Database** window has the current list of objects. To do this, make the window active (select it) and press **F5**.

F5

9 Select Click Options

You can specify whether one click or two clicks opens an object in the **Objects list**. Choose **Tools, Options**, and then click the **View** tab. Under **Click options in database window**, select **Single-click open** or **Double-click open**.

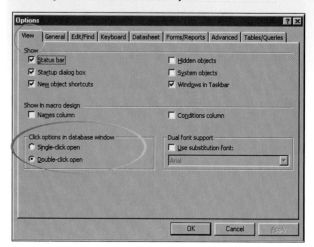

10 Change Object Appearance

Objects can appear in the window in one of four ways. On the **Database** window toolbar, click one of the four buttons to the right of the **Delete** button. When you find your preference, keep that button pressed in.

Small icons——————List

Large icons——————Details

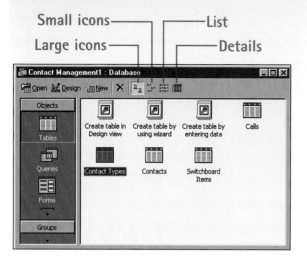

11 Show or Hide Shortcuts

To change the option for showing the shortcuts for creating new database objects, select **Tools, Options** and click the **View** tab. In the **Show** area, select or deselect the check box next to **New object shortcuts**.

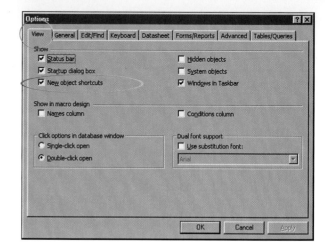

12 View Object Properties

Viewing an object's properties allows you to see information such as the date an object was created and a description of the object. To view this information, right-click the object and choose **Properties** from the shortcut menu.

Right-click

End

How-To Hints

Use the Shortcut Menu

Remember, most of the **Database** window's toolbar commands can also be found on an object's shortcut menu. Right-click an object to see your choices. If right-clicking is easier for you, by all means use it regularly.

Showing Shortcuts for Creating New Objects

As mentioned in Step 11, you can hide the shortcuts for creating new database objects. For example, if you know you won't be creating any new objects (tables, forms, and so on) in your database for some time, you can remove the **Create "Object" in Design view** and **Create "Object" by using wizard** options from the Database window by following the instructions in Step 11.

How to Create a Blank Database

After you've mastered the Access 2000 basics, you'll probably want to build your own database from scratch. Follow these steps to create a blank database.

Begin

1 Start a Blank Database

To start a blank database, choose **File, New** or click the **New** button on the toolbar. On the **General** tab of the **New** dialog box, choose **Database** and click **OK**.

Click

2 Name the Database File

Type a filename in the text box provided in the **File New Database** dialog box. Click **Create**. The **Database** window for your new database appears.

3 Create the Tables

Click the **Tables** button in the Objects bar. Choose one of the create table shortcuts in the **Database** window and create any tables you need for your database. (For more on creating tables, see Part 4, "Creating and Working with Access Tables.")

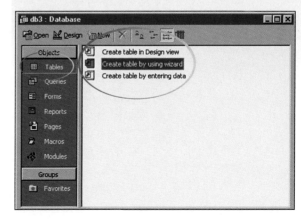

4 Create the Forms

Click the **Forms** button on the Objects bar. Choose one of the create form shortcuts in the **Database** window and create any forms you need for your database. (For more on creating forms, see Part 6.)

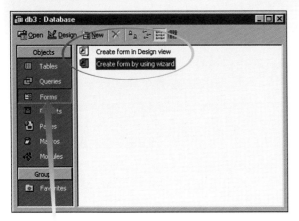

 Click

5 Save Your Data

Access almost always automatically saves any changes in your database. However, it's a good habit to manually save files whenever possible. If the **Save** button is active on the **Database** toolbar, click it to save any changes to your database.

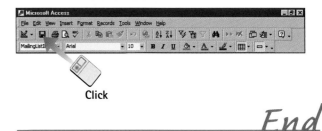

Click

End

How-To Hints

Plan a Database

It's best to sketch out a rough outline for your database before you start building one. Use the outline to help keep you on track with the tables, forms, reports, and other elements you have to create.

Use Database Wizards

Usually, it's easier to create a database using the wizard provided by Microsoft. The wizard contains all the components you need to get your database under way. While you're still new to Access, you may find the wizard easier to use than following an outline for a blank database you build yourself.

How to Add a Database Password

At some point, you will need to keep someone out of a database. Doing so is relatively simple if you use a **password**. However, make sure that you are the one to password protect your database first. If someone else has access to your database, that person can lock you out of your own database. Follow these steps to secure your database from prying eyes.

Begin

1 Close the Database

Close the database you want to secure with a password: Click the **Close** box in the upper-right corner of the **Database** window or choose **File, Close**.

Click

2 The Open Dialog Box

Choose **File, Open** to bring up the **Open** dialog box.

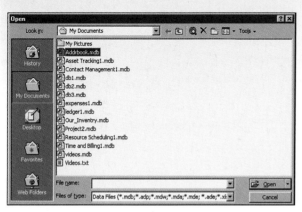

3 Use Open Exclusive

Highlight the filename of the database to be secured. Click the arrow to the right of the **Open** button at the bottom of the dialog box and then choose **Open Exclusive**.

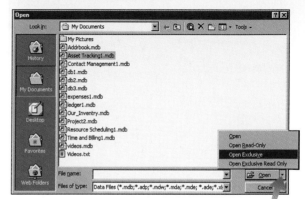

Click

4 Open the Password Dialog Box

When the database opens, choose **Tools, Security, Set Database Password**. The **Set Database Password** dialog box opens.

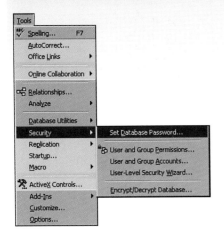

5 Enter the Password

Enter the password you want to assign to this database in the **Password** text box. As you type, notice that Access displays asterisks instead of the letters you type. This additional security feature keeps prying eyes from learning your password as you type it.

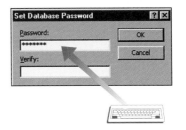

6 Verify and Set the Password

Type the password again in the **Verify** text box and click **OK** to set the password. Your database is now password-secured.

End

How-To Hints

Back Up a Database Before Securing

Before you secure a database with a password, make sure that you create a backup copy using the skills you'll learn later in this part in Task 12, "How to Back Up a Database." Keep the backup in a safe location.

Remember Your Password

An Access database password cannot be recovered. If you lose your password, you will not be able to open the database again.

Passwords Are Case Sensitive

Passwords are case sensitive. That means it makes a difference whether you use uppercase or lowercase letters in your password. Be sure to keep this in mind when making a note of your passwords for Access databases.

How to Delete a Database Password

Just as you will sometimes need to secure a database with a password, there will also be times when you no longer need a password to protect a database. Removing a password from a database is as easy as assigning that password. However, keep in mind that anyone who knows the password can also delete it.

Begin

1 The Open Dialog Box

Choose **File, Open** to display the **Open** dialog box.

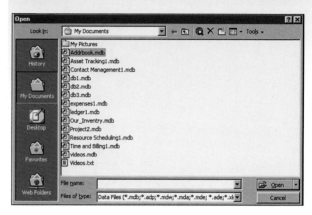

2 Open the Protected Database

Highlight the filename of the database from which you want to remove the password, and then click the **Open** button at the bottom of the **Open** dialog box.

Click

3 Enter the Password

The **Password Required** dialog box opens, asking for your password. Type the password and click **OK**.

4 Choose Unset Database Password

Choose **Tools, Security, Unset Database Password**. The **Unset Database Password** dialog box appears.

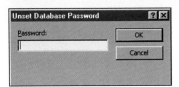

5 Verify the Password

Type the password in the **Password** text box of the **Unset Database Password** dialog box and click **OK**. The password has been removed from the database.

End

How-To Hints

K.I.S.S. (Keep It Simple, Stupid)

The secret to a good password is to keep it simple enough for you to remember, yet difficult enough that nobody else will be able to figure it out. Think of the person who gave you your first kiss, and use his or her middle name rather than your spouse's. A co-worker may not be able to guess your spouse's mother's maiden name, but you can bet that your kid will develop an interest in genealogy if that's what it takes to get to the data you're trying to keep hidden!

How to Close a Database

The last thing you do in your day-to-day work with a database is close it. Access offers you several ways to close your databases.

Begin

1 Activate the Database

Activate the database you want to close by clicking its button on the Windows taskbar. You can't close an Access database if Microsoft Word is in the active window!

Click

2 Save Any Changes

Access almost always automatically saves any changes in your database. However, it's a good habit to manually save files whenever possible. Click the **Save** button (if it's active) on the Database toolbar to save any changes that Access hasn't automatically saved.

Click

3 Use the Close Box

Click the **Close** box in the upper-right corner of the **Database** window to close the active database.

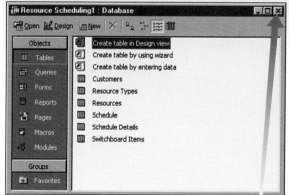

Click

4 Use the File Menu

An alternative to closing a database with the **Close** box is to choose **File, Close**.

5 Close by Exiting Access

If you're through working in Access and want to cut down on steps, click the **Close** box in the upper-right corner of the main Access window.

Click

6 Exit Using the Menu Bar

An alternative to exiting Access and any open database at the same time is to choose **File, Exit**.

How-To Hints

Can I Save My Data?

Access 2000 saves any tables, forms, and so on as you close them. It's best, however, to get into the habit of saving your changes manually by clicking the **Save** button on the toolbar whenever possible. If the **Save** button is grayed out, you'll know that Access has saved everything, and all your data is safe. If the Save button is not grayed out, click it to preserve vulnerable data.

End

How to Compact a Database

Compacting your Access database helps it run more efficiently by eliminating fragmented disk space used by the database and by keeping your records updated.

1 Compact the Current Database

With the database you want to compact open, choose **Tools, Database Utilities, Compact and Repair Database**. The database is compacted. The length of time it takes to compact varies depending on the size of the database. It's best to wait for the compact procedure to complete before you attempt to do any work in the database.

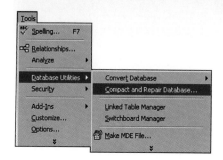

2 Compact a Closed Database

To compact a closed database, first close *all* databases. Choose **Tools, Database Utilities, Compact and Repair Database**.

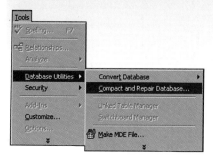

3 Choose a Database

In the **Database to Compact From** dialog box, select the filename of the database you want to compact. Click **Compact**.

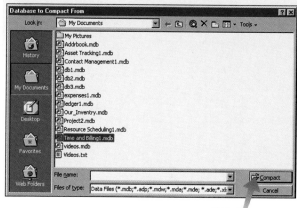

Click

4 Select a Filename

The **Compact Database Into** dialog box appears. Choose the filename that the database will have after it is compacted. You can choose the same filename as the original file. Click **Save**.

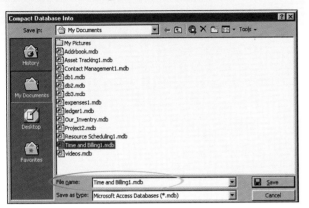

5 Confirm the Overwrite

If you selected the same filenames in the **Database to Compact From** and **Compact Database Into** dialog boxes, you are asked whether you want to replace the existing file. Click **Yes**.

Click

End

How-To Hints

Compact a Database Automatically When You Close It

You can choose to have your databases compacted automatically every time you close them: Choose **Tools, Options**. On the **General** tab, click the **Compact On Close** check box.

Stop Compacting

If you want to stop a database from being compacted, press **Ctrl+Break+Esc**.

When to Compact

It's a good idea to compact a database after you have deleted large amounts of data or many database objects. If you don't compact at this time, the database can become fragmented and may perform more slowly and inefficiently.

When to Use Different Filenames

In general, you can use the same filename for the database in its uncompacted and compacted states. For critical data, you may want to assign a different filename to the compacted database in case your computer crashes during the compact process.

How to Back Up a Database

Backing up your database files should be a regularly scheduled task. You never know when a file may be corrupted or damaged. Although this task doesn't cover all the ways to back up files, it does give you a good start on one way to get the job done.

Begin

1 Open My Computer

Make sure that the database you want to back up is closed and then double-click the **My Computer** icon on your desktop to access your file directories.

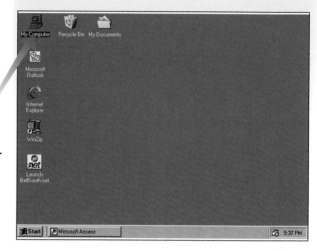

Double-click

2 Browse to the File

Browse through the folders to find the database you want to back up. (The example here shows the Windows 98 Internet Explorer interface.)

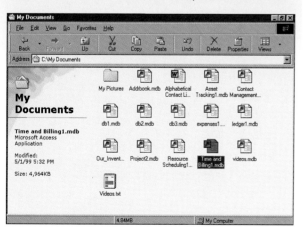

3 Copy the File

Right-click the file you want to back up and select **Copy** from the shortcut menu.

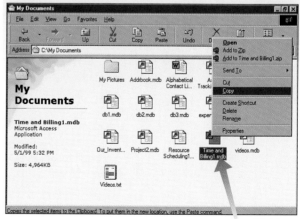

Right-click

4 Browse to the Backup Folder

Browse to the folder in which you want to place the copy of your database file.

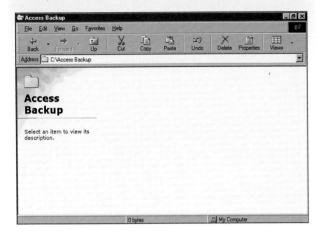

5 Paste the File

Right-click an area of the folder window without an icon and select **Paste** from the shortcut menu.

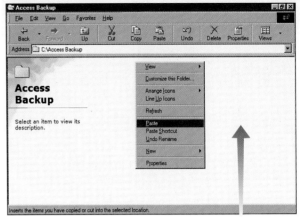

Right-click

6 Confirm the Overwrite

If you've backed up the database before into the same folder, you'll see a dialog box asking you to confirm that you want to overwrite the existing file. Click **Yes**. Your database is now backed up and safe in the backup folder.

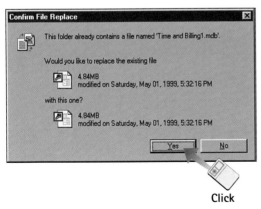

Click

End

How-To Hints

Back Up to Media

You can back up your files to floppies or a zip drive. When you're backing up to floppies and your files are larger than 1.44 MB, use a backup program such as Microsoft Backup so that you can use more than one floppy. Such programs divide the backup files into sizes appropriate for the floppies you are using and prompt you to insert another disk.

Keep a Dedicated Backup Folder

Create a folder called **Backups** somewhere on your hard drive. This should be the folder to which you always back up your files. The confusion saved is well worth the disk space you spend.

How to Preview a Database File Before Printing

Previewing a database file before you print it could save you some time, paper, and ink. When you use the **Preview** command, you see onscreen what will print. You can therefore make corrections to your printing options or to the database data before you actually use up your printer ink.

Begin

1 Highlight the Object

In the **Database** window's **Objects list**, click the name of the object you want to preview.

2 Open the Preview

To open the preview window, choose **File, Print Preview**.

3 Use the Zoom Box

If the preview is too small or too large for you to comfortably see, select the appropriate option in the **Zoom** box. Alternatively, left-click when the cursor is shaped like a magnifying glass to enlarge or reduce the view.

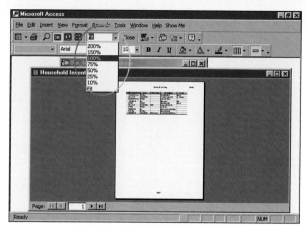

4 Preview Two Pages

If you want to see two pages at once during the preview, click the **Two Pages** button on the toolbar.

Click

5 Preview Multiple Pages

To preview several pages at once, click the **Multiple Pages** button on the toolbar and drag your mouse across the number of pages you want to view. Release the mouse button when you have selected the correct number of pages.

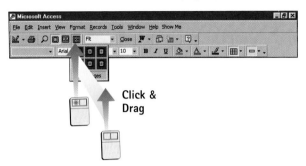

Click & Drag

6 Close Print Preview

Click the **Close** button on the toolbar to close the **Print Preview** window.

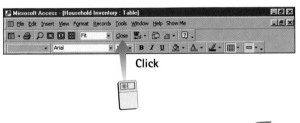

Click

End

How-To Hints

The Semi-Paperless Office

This book is proof that the predictions about computers and a paperless society are far from reality. However, you *can* use Print Preview to cut down on the amount of paper that rolls off your printer. Use Print Preview to verify that your report or other information is complete and will appear as you intend before you use the Print command. If you only want to print partial information and don't want to take the time to hide fields or perform a query to isolate that information, use Print Preview to pick a page from a group of pages and find out which page number to prompt for the printout.

How to Print Database Objects

Eventually, you'll want to print a table, report, form, or some other object from your database. Turn your printer on and follow these steps.

Begin

1 Highlight the Object

In the **Database** window, select the object you want to print from the **Objects bar** and the **Objects list**.

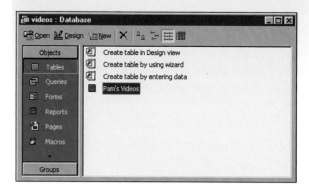

2 Preview the Object

As explained in Task 13, "How to Preview a Database File Before Printing," choose **File, Print Preview** to see how the object will look in printed form.

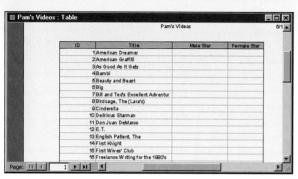

3 Close the Preview

Close the preview window by clicking the **Close** button on the toolbar.

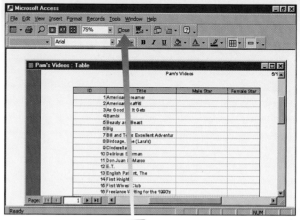

Click

4 Set Up the Page

If you have to change options for paper size, margins, or page orientation, open the object again and choose **File, Page Setup**. Make your selections and click **OK**.

Click

5 Choose File, Print

Choose **File, Print**. Choosing to print from the menu options (rather than clicking the Print button in the toolbar) allows you to change any printer options in the **Print** dialog box.

6 Select Print Options

In the **Print** dialog box, make your selections for printer options such as resolution, print range, and the number of copies you want to print. Click **OK**. Your document will now print.

How-To Hints

The Print Button on the Toolbar

Of course, you can always click the **Print** button on the toolbar to print a document. If you do, be aware that you will get only one copy of the document, printed on the default printer with the default printer options. When you choose **File, Print** to open the **Print** dialog box, you can change some of those default settings.

End

Task

4

Creating and Working with Access Tables

*I*n this part of the book, you'll learn about the *table*—the spreadsheet-style document known as a *datasheet* in Access. Tables are the storage containers for the information you enter into Access. Each table consists of *fields* (columns) of data; a collection of fields (each row) makes up a *record*.

The number of tables you can have in a database is limited only by the amount of hard drive (storage) space you have available on your computer or network. But no matter how many tables you have, they are all saved as part of the database itself.

There are ways you can help Access improve your database's speed and efficiency. Data types and input masks not only ease data entry by establishing specific data entry formats (for example, a **Yes/No** Data Type check box or a phone number mask), they let Access know that it only needs to provide a set amount of space in the field size.

In addition to manually keying in each record, you can also *import* data from another source (such as a text file created in Word that probably won't ever change). Because Access generally works faster with its own tables, importing means that you can move data to Access quickly and then modify it within Access and not worry about slowing things down. On the other hand, you *link* data if the data you need to use in the Access database may also be updated in a program other than Access. When you link data, changes are made to both the source file and the Access file. Although Access may operate a little slower because of such a link, you still save time compared to making changes to several separate files stored in different locations.

If you're working on a network and you have any doubts about what you're changing, check with the System Administrator before you make any changes to the database. Don't *assume* that user-level protection safeguards are in place—*verify* that they are. ●

How to Create a Table with the Table Wizard

Access comes with wizards that make it easy to create tables. The **Table Wizard** provides required fields and suggestions for optional fields, and then sets the data types for those fields. In Step 5 of this task, look at the **Table** choices the wizard provides: There are personal database tables (such as address books, recipes, exercise logs, and "collections"). For business operations, there are mailing lists and the usual client- or customer-related tables as well as two tables for students and classes.

2 Create a Table from Within Access

With Access open, click the **New** icon on the **Access** toolbar. In the **Startup** dialog box, select **Blank Access database** and click **OK**.

Click

Begin

1 Open Access to Create a Table

If Access is already open and you want to create a table in a new database, skip Step 1 and go to Step 2. To open Access from the **Start** menu, choose **Programs, Microsoft Access**. From the **Startup** dialog box, select **Blank Access database** and click **OK**. Skip to Step 3.

Click

3 Enter a Filename

In the **File New Database** dialog box, type the filename of the database you want to create. In this example, type **04task01**. Access automatically adds the .MDB file extension. Click **Create**.

4 Start the Wizard

Access opens with the **Tables** option selected in the Objects bar in the left pane of the **04task01 : Database** window. In the right pane, double-click the icon next to **Create table by using wizard**.

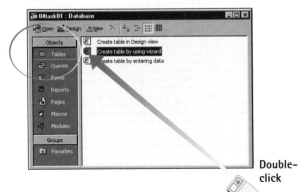

Double-click

5 Choose the Category

The Table Wizard gives you a choice of **Business** and **Personal** categories, each with a number of sample tables. Click an item in the **Sample Tables** list. For this example, select **Business**, **Contacts**. (Notice that the **Sample Fields** list changes based on the table you select.)

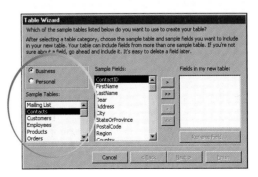

6 Pick Fields

From the **Sample Fields** list, select the fields you want to include in this table. To select and add fields one at a time, click the field name to highlight it and click the single arrow (>) button to move the field to the **Fields in my new table** list. To select all the fields, click the double arrow (>>) button. As you'll learn in Task 12, "How to Insert and Move a Field," you can add fields later if you decide that you need them. Likewise, you can delete a field if you find that it isn't necessary.

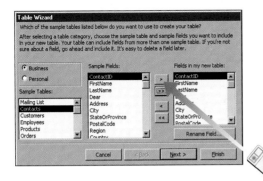

Click

7 Select a Field to Rename

After you select your fields, you can choose to rename a field. Select the field you want to rename from the list in the **Fields in my new table** pane and click **Rename Field**. In this example, select the **Photograph** field and rename it **OnlineNick**. (You know you won't include photographs in this database, but you *do* deal with people who go by online nicknames, which can vary from their email names.)

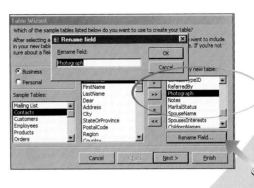

Click

Continues

How to Create a Table with the Table Wizard Continued

8 Rename the Field with the Wizard

In the **Rename field** dialog box, type the new field name and click **OK**.

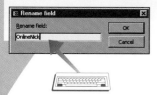

9 The Renamed Field

The new field name appears in the **Fields in my new table** list. Click **Next**.

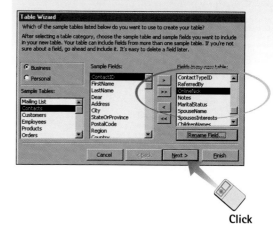

Click

10 Name the Table

The Table Wizard asks **What do you want to name your table?** (This name is different than the filename you assigned earlier.) Click in the box and type the table name.

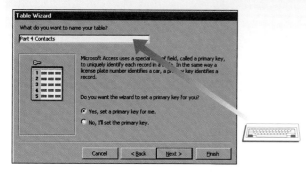

11 Set the Primary Key

You can either let Access set a primary key or set one yourself. (Refer to the Glossary for a definition of *primary key*.) You also work with primary keys in Task 3 later in this part.) Select **Yes, set a primary key for me** and click **Next**.

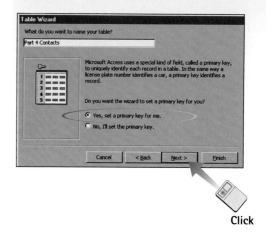

Click

12 Let the Wizard Create the Table

The wizard now has the information it needs to create the table. Make sure that the **Enter data directly into the table** option is selected and click **Finish**. (Later, you can use the Form Wizard, available from the **Objects** bar's **Forms** list in the **Database** window, to create a form to help you enter data.)

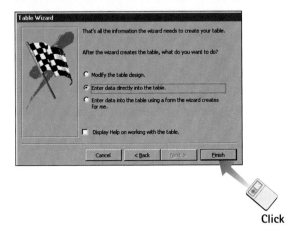

Click

13 Look at the New Table

Access creates the table and displays the **Table** window. Notice the **ContactsID** field; this is the primary key field that Access created for you in Step 11. Scroll across the window to view all the fields you added in Steps 6 through 9.

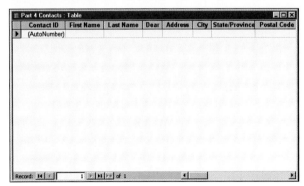

End

How-To Hints

Click Options

Remember that when you're instructed to double-click, it's with the assumption that double-click is still set as your Open Object option.

An Object's Shortcut Menu

Throughout Part 4, you make frequent use of an object's **shortcut menu**—the one that appears when you right-click an object.

TASK 2

How to Create a Table on Your Own

For a simple table (one with only a few fields), it is sometimes easier to create your own table rather than use the wizard.

Begin

1 Create a Table in Design View

With a database open and the **Database** window active onscreen, choose **Tables** from the Objects bar. In the right pane, double-click the icon next to **Create table in Design view**.

Double-click

2 Enter Fields and Data Types

On the first line under **Field Name**, type the name of the field you want to add to the table (**ExampleOnly**) and press **Tab**. From the **Data Type** column, press **Tab** again. In the **Description** column, type any notes to yourself regarding the field you are defining.

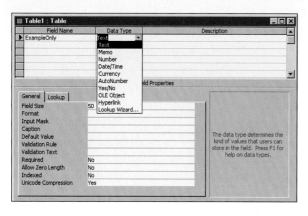

3 Save the Table

Repeat Step 2 to define additional fields for the table. When you're done entering field information, exit the window. Access asks whether you want to save the changes to your table. Click **Yes** and enter the name you want to assign to the table (**Part 4 Task 2**). Click **Yes** to let Access assign the primary key. (Access 2000 creates a field called **ID** with **AutoNumber** as its data type; Access assigns the primary key to this field.) The table now appears in the **Database** window.

4 Create a Table in Spreadsheet Mode

Perhaps you like to see the spreadsheet-style information in front of you as you work. To create a table and work in that mode, double-click the icon next to **Create table by entering data** in the **Database** window.

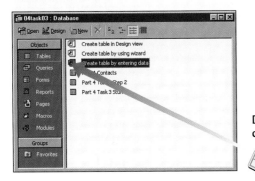

Double-click

5 The Table with Unnamed Fields

Access opens an as-yet unnamed table in Datasheet view with the cursor positioned, ready for you to begin entering data. (Task 3 covers how to rename fields.) Type some sample data, pressing **Tab** to move between fields.

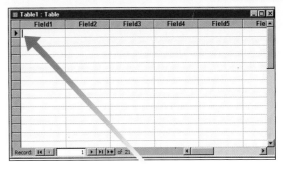

6 Save Your Work

Exit the table by clicking the **Close button** in the upper-right corner. When you're asked whether you want to save your work, click **Yes**. Type a name for the table (**Part 4 Task 2 Step 6**) and click **OK**. When you're prompted to let Access assign the primary key, click **Yes**. The new table appears in the **Database** window.

End

How-To Hints

Data Types

Access uses the **Text** data type in the **Data Type** column when you create a field in Design view. **Text** is the default data type for all columns when you create a table by entering data in Datasheet view. To change the data type, switch to Design view, move to the **Data Type** column, click the down-arrow button, and select from the list.

Data types include **Text** (up to 255 characters), **Memo** (lengthy text up to 64,000 characters), **Number, Date/Time, Currency, AutoNumber** (for automatically numbered sequential records), **Yes/No, OLE Object** (up to 1 gigabyte, limited by disk space), **Hyperlink,** and **Lookup Wizard** (used to choose a value from another table or list).

How to Customize Access Tables

Even a wizard can't predict every database scenario. Therefore, at some point you'll probably want to make changes to the tables you create. This task gives you some suggestions for customizing the tables you have created.

Begin

1 Rename a Table

To rename a table, right-click the table name in the **Database** window's Objects list and select **Rename**. (This example uses one of the tables you created in Task 2: **Part 4 Task 2 Step 6**). Type the new table name (**Part 4 Task 3 Stuff**) and press **Enter**.

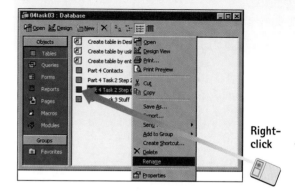

Right-click

2 Rename a Field in Datasheet View

Open the table in Datasheet view (double-click the table name in the **Database** window). Move the mouse cursor over the field bars at the top of the table until the pointer changes to a down arrow, and then click to select that field. Right-click the field and select **Rename Column** from the menu.

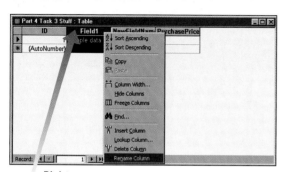

Right-click

3 Rename a Field in Datasheet View, Option 2

Open the table in Datasheet view and double-click the field bar at the top of the window. Backspace to erase the original field name and then type in the new one. Press **Enter** when you're done.

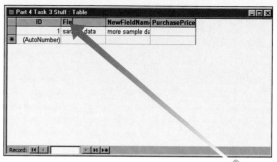

Double-click

4 Open the Table in Design View

Open the table in Design view by selecting the table from the Objects list in the **Database** window and clicking the **Design** button on the **Database** window toolbar.

 Click

5 Rename a Field in Design View

Double-click the entry you want to rename in the **Field Name** column in Design view. Type the new field name to replace the old one.

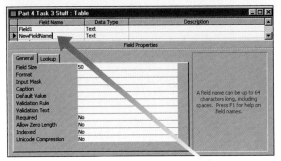

 Double-click

6 Set or Change the Primary Key

Access uses the primary key to reference this table to other tables. To set or change a primary key, right-click the name of the field you want to make the primary key. From the shortcut menu, select **Primary Key**. (Notice that the key icon moves from any previously selected field to the new field.) Alternatively, select the field and then click the **Primary Key** button on the **Access** toolbar.

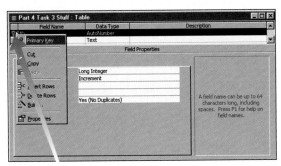

 Right-click

Continues

How-To Hints

Some Things Aren't Chiseled in Stone

Change your mind about a field or table name you've renamed but can't recall the original name? If you act immediately, you can undo the change by selecting **Edit, Undo** from the menu bar or by pressing **Ctrl+Z**.

Change Views in Open Tables

You can switch between views when the table is open, too. In Datasheet view, click the **View** toolbar button to switch to Design view (in Datasheet view, the **View** button displays the design icon). In Design view, click the **View** toolbar button to switch to Datasheet view (in Design view, the **View** button displays the datasheet icon).

7 Set or Change Field Properties

With the table open in Design view, you can customize field entries. For example, if you add a **PurchasePrice** field to a table, you *could* use the default **Text** data type. However, it's more practical to select the **Currency** data type because it adds the decimal information for you. (Refer to Task 2 for more about data types. See Task 6, "How to Use Input Masks," for more data format information.)

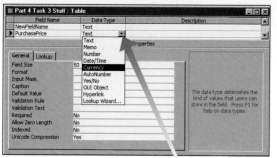

Click

8 Adjust the Column Width

To adjust the width of the column so that all the text in the column can be seen, right-click anywhere in the column and select **Column Width** from the menu. Make the appropriate selections from the dialog box and click **OK**.

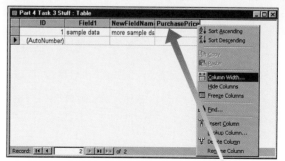

Right-click

9 Hide a Column

You can display a table in Datasheet view with only some of the columns visible. Right-click the field name of the column you want to hide, select **Column Width**, and set the width to **0** (zero) to hide the column. Or select the field name and choose **Format, Hide Columns**. Or right-click the field name and select **Hide Columns**. (Bring back the columns by selecting **Format, Unhide Columns**.)

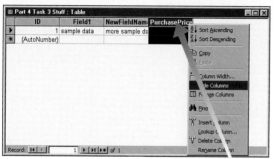

Right-click

10 Freeze a Column

You can make a column (or columns) stay on the screen regardless of where you scroll in your table. In Datasheet view, right-click the column you want to freeze on the screen and select **Freeze Columns**. (To unfreeze columns, select **Format, Unfreeze All Columns**.)

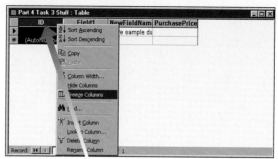

Right-click

11 Sort in A-to-Z Order

To display information in A-to-Z or 0-to-9 (lowest-to-highest) order in a column in Datasheet view, right-click anywhere in the column and select **Sort Ascending**. Alternatively, position the cursor anywhere in the column and click the **Sort Ascending** button on the toolbar.

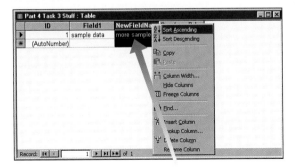

Right-click

12 Sort in Z-to-A Order

To display information in Z-to-A or 9-to-0 (highest-to-lowest) order in a column in Datasheet view, right-click anywhere in the column and select **Sort Descending**. Alternatively, position the cursor anywhere in the column and click the **Sort Descending** button on the **Database** toolbar.

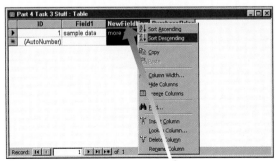

Right-click

End

How-To Hints

Selecting Multiple Columns

To select more than one column, position the mouse pointer over a field name until it changes to the **Column Field Selector** (what we refer to as the *down arrow*). Then drag the mouse across the remaining fields you want to select.

Specifying Column Widths

In Datasheet view, to set the column width to a specific number of *twips* (an Access measurement equal to 1/20th of a point or 1/1440th of an inch), right-click the field name whose width you want to adjust and select **Column Width**. To let Access adjust the column to accommodate the amount of data in the field, click **Best Fit**.

Adjusting Column Width Manually

You can manually adjust a column's width in Datasheet view by moving the mouse to the right of the field name until it changes to the Horizontal Resize pointer (a vertical line with left and right arrows). Drag the line to the desired width or double-click the right border to adjust the width to the longest line of text in the column.

How to Enter Data into a Table

All the pretty tables and beautifully formatted forms you create won't mean a whole lot without any data in them to make them relevant. You can input information in a number of ways so that after it leaves your fingertips by way of the keyboard, it's available at your fingertips using a database query or report.

Begin

1 Type in Datasheet View

In Datasheet view, click the field in which you want to enter data. All toolbar editing options (such as cut, copy, and paste—see Step 3) are available in this view. When you finish typing, press **Tab** or an arrow key to reposition the cursor where you want to type next.

Click

2 Use a Form

Forms isolate each record for you. We'll cover how to enter data using a form in Part 6, "Creating and Working with Access Forms." After you enter data using the form, you can exit the form and return to the table or select Datasheet view.

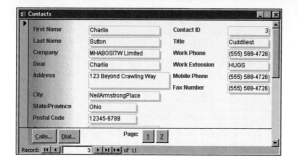

3 Cut or Copy and Paste

There may be times when it's simpler to cut (**Ctrl+X**) or copy (**Ctrl+C**) and paste (**Ctrl+V**) information from one record to another. You cut data from one spot and move it to another. You copy and paste to duplicate information.

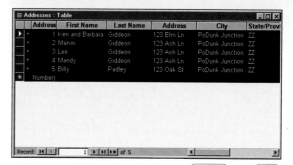

Ctrl + X
Ctrl + V
Ctrl + C

4 Drop-Down Data Entry

You can save yourself repetitive typing. For example, your address book probably has several categories of contacts—business, friends, church—or maybe you know a number of people named *Smith*. After you give your form a drop-down list, double-click the entry window to add other items to the multiple data choices.

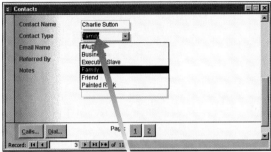

 Double-click

5 Paste the Records

You can copy a record from one table and paste the entire record in another table that has matching fields. Select the entire record and choose **Edit, Copy**. Then select an appropriate row in the same table (or another table) and choose **Edit, Paste**. (See Project 5, "Working with an Access Table.")

6 Use a Wizard to Import

When Access imports data from another source, it makes a copy of the original data and inserts it into your table. You'll use a wizard to import data in Task 10 later in this part, and you'll learn how to import text in Project 5.

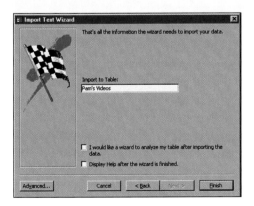

End

How-To Hints

Skip to a New Record

On the **Access** toolbar, click **New Record** (the button with the right arrow and the asterisk) to move to the area to where you type the data for a new entry.

List Box Data Entry

A **drop-down list box** (the purpose of which is to save time during data entry and to help ensure accuracy) has one value until you expand it to show more. You can view an example of this kind of box in the **Inventry.mdb** (household inventory) sample database: Open the database, and from the **Main Switchboard**, select **Enter/View Household Inventory Items**. Click the down arrow next to **bedroom** to see the "room" choices. To learn more about list box data entry, see *Using Microsoft Access 2000* (published by Que Corporation).

How to Establish Table Relationships

Relationships put the *relations* (defined associations) in a relational database. The relationship is defined by a common field that appears in both tables.

Access displays records in other tables related to a record in the open table in *subdatasheets*. In Datasheet view, you see plus marks (+) to the left of records that have related data. Click the + to display the subdatasheet (related records); click the resulting – to hide that information again.

Begin

1 Define a Table Relationship

This task uses the **Asset Tracking** database created using a wizard. To define a relationship (add a new one), close any tables you may have open. Switch to the **Database** window and click the **Relationships** button on the **Access** toolbar.

Click

2 Show Tables

If you need to add a table to the relationship, right-click anywhere in the **Relationships** window. From the shortcut menu, choose **Show Table**. The connecting lines show the fields through which one table relates to another.

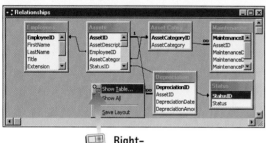

Right-click

3 Add Tables

In the **Show Table** dialog box, select the name of the table you want to add to the **Relationships** window and click **Add**. Add as many tables as you want and then click **Close**.

Click

4 Link the Tables

The easiest way to relate two tables is to click the field that's common to both in the first table and drag the mouse to the same field in the second table. When you release the mouse button, the **Edit Relationships** dialog box appears.

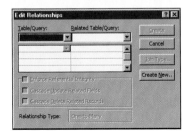

5 Create a New Relationship

Click the **Create New** button to open the **Create New** dialog box, from which you can define your left and right table and column names by making choices from the drop-down lists. Click **OK** when you're done.

Click

6 Edit an Existing Relationship

To edit an existing relationship, double-click the line connecting two tables in the **Relationships** window. The **Edit Relationships** dialog box opens, and you can make your changes.

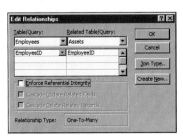

End

How-To Hints

Don't Panic!

In most cases, when you create a table or a database with the help of a wizard, Access defines the relationships for you.

If, on the other hand, you're working with a new table you created without the help of a wizard and no relationships are yet defined, the **Show Table** dialog box opens when you click the **Relationships** button on the **Access** toolbar.

Types of Relationships

There are three types of relationships: one-to-one (each record in the first table relates to only one record in the second table), one-to-many (each record in the first table can relate to many or no records in the second table), and many-to-many (a record in either table can relate to a number of records in the other table). Many-to-many relationships are handled through *junction tables*, which break the many-to-many relationships down into the necessary number of one-to-many relationships to keep it all straight—which, as you may have determined, is far beyond the scope of this book!

How to Use Input Masks

In addition to the data type choices you learned about in Task 3, input masks are another way to control the format of your table data. An input mask controls how the data is entered. For example, if you attempt to enter data the wrong way (such as in all caps instead of in lowercase letters), Access won't let you.

Begin

1 Use the Asset Tracking Database

This task uses the **Asset Tracking** database as it's created by the Access 2000 wizard. Open the database, minimize the Main Switchboard, and maximize the **Database** window. In the Objects bar, click **Tables**. Select the **Employees** table and click **Open** on the **Database** window toolbar.

Click

2 Look at an Input Mask

To select or change an input mask, the table must be in Design view (which you could have selected from the **Database** window toolbar). However, before you switch to that view, click the cell under the **Work Phone** field heading. Notice that (___) ___-____ appears in the cell. That's an example of an input mask: It ensures the format in which the data is entered (in this case, the phone number). Now click the **View** button on the **Access** toolbar to switch to Design view.

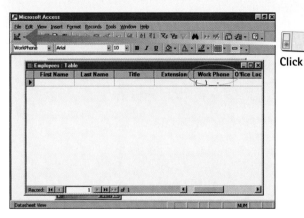

Click

3 Select the Field for the Mask

In the top half of the Design view window, select the field for which you want to define an input mask (in this case, the **Extension** field). In the lower half of the window, click the **Input Mask** property field. Click the **build** button (the three periods) that appears to the right of that line.

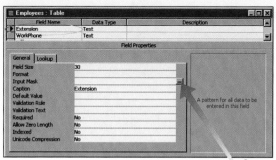

Click

4 The Input Mask Wizard

The **Input Mask Wizard** asks you to select the format that matches how you want the data in your field to look. Select **Extension** and click **Next**.

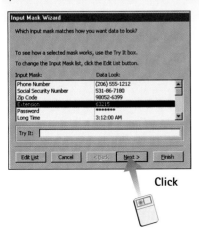

Click

5 Format the Input Mask

In the **Input Mask** text box, type the appropriate number of characters for the extension number in the format needed. You can also insert any special characters that might be needed (for example, if you want to draw attention to some extension switchboard numbers, such as 9-9999).

6 Test the Input Mask

A *placeholder character* is what is shown onscreen when you type in the actual data. From the **Placeholder character** drop-down list in the wizard window, select the character you want. Click in the **Try It** box at the bottom of the wizard screen and test your mask. Click **Finish** when you're satisfied with the result.

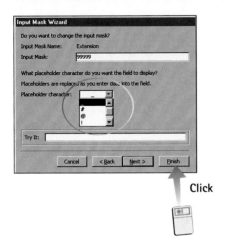

Click

How-To Hints

Better Safe Than Sorry
Back up your database before you make design changes. That way you "can go home again" without a lot of fuss if you don't like the changes.

Placeholder to Value
When you enter data in a field that contains an input mask, Access replaces the empty (placeholder) characters with the values you enter.

Keeping It All Straight
Your data type choices restrict how data is entered in a field. The input mask forces you to follow rules as you enter the data.

End

How to Create an Input Mask

Those of you who still frown on wizards and automation probably aren't using a database any-how. No, seriously! If you find it simpler to write your own input mask instead of using a wizard to create one, Access allows for that route, too.

Begin

1 Open the Asset Tracking Employees Table

This task uses the **Asset Tracking** database as it's created by the Access 2000 wizard. Open the data-base, minimize the Main Switchboard, and maximize the **Database** window. In the Objects bar, click **Tables**. Select the **Employees** table and click the **Design** toolbar button.

Click

2 Select the Field for the Mask

In the top half of the Design view win-dow, select the field for which you want to define an input mask (in this case, the **Extension** field). In the lower half of the window, click the **Input Mask** property field. (If an input mask is already defined on the line, select it and press **Backspace** or **Delete** to rid of it.)

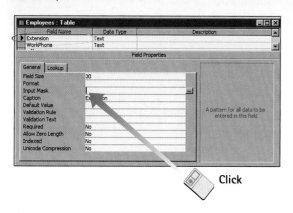

Click

3 Type the Input Mask Formula

Type the formula **9\-9999;;** (ending with two semicolons). This input mask formula defines one number followed by a hyphen and four more numbers. You've left the second definition blank (the reason there are two semicolons side by side) so that Access stores the literal value and not the hyphenat-ed value. You've also left the third area blank so that Access uses the default placeholder character, the underline (_).

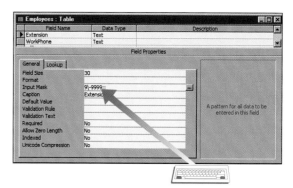

4 Look at the Input Mask

Click the **View** button on the **Access** toolbar to change to Datasheet view. Click **Yes** when you're asked if you want to save the changes to the table. Click the empty cell underneath the **Extension** field to see how the input mask appears.

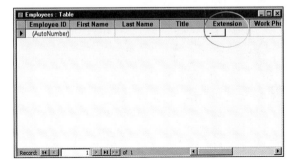

5 Change the Placeholder

On the **Access** toolbar, click the **View** button to return to Design view. On the line on which you typed your input mask in Step 3, add one of the following characters to the end of the mask formula: **#, @, !, $, %,** or *****. The character you type is used as the placeholder. Choose the **@** character so that your mask formula is now **9\-9999;;@**.

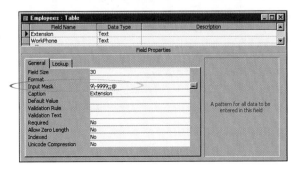

6 A Whole New Look

Repeat Step 4 to see how the input mask appears now.

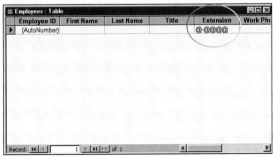

End

How-To Hints

How to Define an Input Mask

An input mask definition can contain up to three sections, which are separated by semi-colons (**;**):

- ✓ The first part is the input mask itself.

- ✓ The second part determines whether the table stores the literal value. A **0** sets the table to store literal characters (including hyphens and other formatting characters); a **1** or a blank tells the table to store only the characters entered in the blanks.

- ✓ The third part specifies a placeholder character for fill-in-the-blank type fields. If you leave this section blank (as you did in Step 3), Access uses the default (_).

Valid Input Mask Characters

Microsoft Access interprets characters in the first part of the **Input Mask** property definition as shown in the following table. To define a literal character, enter any character (other than those shown in the table), including spaces and symbols. To define one of the following characters as a literal character, precede that character with a backslash (\).

Character	Description
0	Digit (0 through 9, entry required; plus (+) and minus (–) signs not allowed).
9	Digit or space (entry not required; plus and minus signs not allowed).
#	Digit or space (entry not required; blank positions converted to spaces, plus and minus signs allowed).
L	Letter (A through Z, entry required).
?	Letter (A through Z, entry optional).
A	Letter or digit (entry required).
a	Letter or digit (entry optional).
&	Any character or a space (entry required).
C	Any character or a space (entry optional).
. , : ; - /	Decimal placeholder and thousands, date, and time separators. (The actual character used depends on the regional settings specified by double-clicking **Regional Settings** in the Windows Control Panel.)
<	Causes all characters that follow to be converted to lowercase.
>	Causes all characters that follow to be converted to uppercase.
!	Causes the input mask to be displayed from right to left, rather than from left to right. Characters typed into the mask always fill it from left to right. You can include the exclamation point anywhere in the input mask.
\	Causes the character that follows to be displayed as a literal character. Used to display any of the characters listed in this table as literal characters (for example, \A is displayed as just A).
Password	Setting the **Input Mask** property to the word **Password** creates a password entry text box. Any character typed in the text box is stored as the character but is displayed as an asterisk (*).

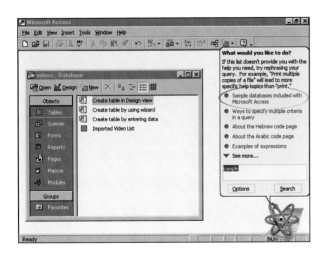

Installing the Sample Databases

The easiest way to install the sample databases that come with Access 2000 is to let the Help system lend a hand. Click the Office Assistant (or choose **Microsoft Office Help** from the **Help** menu). In the **Type your question here, and then click Search** box, type **sample** and click **Search**. From the **What would you like to do?** choices, select **Sample databases included with Microsoft Access**.

How-To Hints

Hyperlink-Assisted Installation

To automatically install any of the sample databases, put your Microsoft Office 2000 CD-ROM in the drive and scroll through the choices described in the Microsoft Access Help description to locate the database you want to install (for example, the **Household Inventory application**). Click the **install and open the applications** hyperlink.

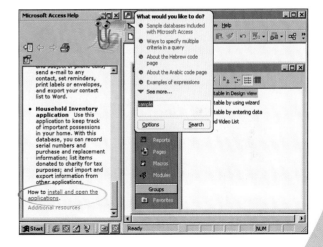

How to Create Indexes for a Table

You can often speed up the search and sort performance of a database if you index fields that have mostly unique values. For example, Access 2000 automatically indexes the primary key for a table. Because adding an index to a field is a complex concept, we recommend that you read *Using Microsoft Access 2000* (published by Que Corporation). In this task, we work with the Wizard-generated **Asset Tracking** database, which already has indexes set up. After following along with these steps, you don't have to save the changes to the sample database: Just choose **No** when the program asks whether you want to save the changes.

Begin

1 Open the Database and Select the Table

Open the database (remember that we're using the Wizard-generated **Asset Tracking** database in this task) and display the **Database** window. Click **Tables** in the Objects bar and select the table you want to index. With the table selected, click the **Design** button on the **Database** toolbar to open the table in Design view.

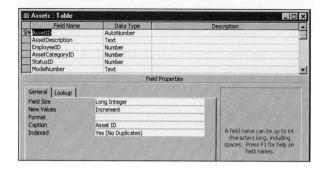

3 Add the Index

On the **General** tab in the bottom half of the window, click the **Indexed** property box. Click the arrow at the end of the text box. To add or change an index, select **Yes (Duplicates OK)** or **Yes (No Duplicates)**. Choose the latter option if you want to ensure that no two records have the same data in this field. Close the **Table** window and click **Yes** to save the index in the table; click **No** if you want to preserve the original database.

2 Select the Field

In the top half of the **Table** window, select the field you want to index. In this example, we chose the **EmployeeID** field. As you'll see in Step 3, this field is already indexed.

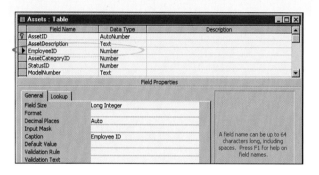

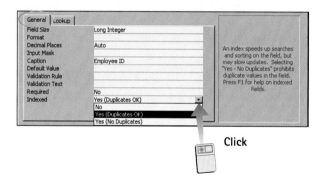

Click

4 Define a Multiple-Field Index

As you did in Step 1, select **Tables** from the Objects bar in the **Database** window and select the table you want to index. Click **Design** on the **Database** toolbar to open the table in Design view.

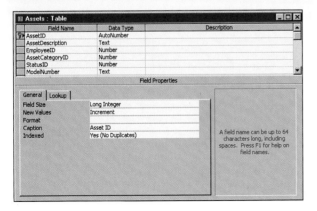

5 Open the Indexes Dialog Box

On the **Access** toolbar, click the **Indexes** button to open the **Indexes: [name of your table]** dialog box.

Click

6 Create the Multiple-Field Index

In the first column of the first line, type the name of the index. (Note that Access uses the field name as the index name, too.) In the second column, select the field you want to use for the index from the drop-down list. In the third column, select the sort order. Click the second line if you want to add another field to the index (for example, you can index the **Last Name** field and then index the **First Name** field). You can have up to 10 fields in an index; the **Assets** table already has 6. Click the **Close box** to close the **Indexes** dialog box when you're done.

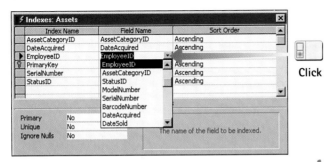

Click

End

How to Edit or Delete an Index

An index can sometimes hinder rather than help. You may set out to improve the speed of your queries, creating indexes expressly for that purpose, only to find that an index creates more problems than it solves. Experiment and use the tried and true backup-first rule, because an index that shaves a second off a query yet slows down data entry (or prevents more than one user on a network at a time from making changes) isn't really efficient.

Begin

1 Open the Indexed Table

Open a database (in this task, we're using the Wizard-generated **Asset Tracking** database) and display the **Database** window. Click **Tables** in the Objects bar and select the table whose index you want to modify. With the table selected, click the **Design** button on the **Database** toolbar to open the table in Design view.

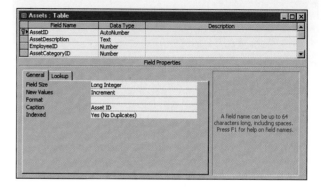

2 Open the Indexes Dialog Box

On the **Access** toolbar, click the **Indexes** button to open the **Indexes** dialog box.

Click

3 Edit the Index

In the **Indexes** dialog box, make any edits or additions required. For example, you can change the index name or add other fields to the index. When you have made your changes, close the **Indexes** dialog box. Close the **Table** window and click **Yes** to save the changes.

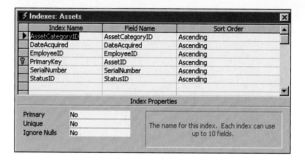

4 Get Ready to Delete an Index

As you did in Step 1, select **Tables** from the Objects bar in the **Database** window and select the table whose index you want to delete. Click **Design** in the **Database** toolbar to open the table in Design view.

Click

5 Open the Indexes Dialog Box

On the **Access** toolbar, click the **Indexes** button to open the **Indexes** dialog box.

Click

6 Delete an Index

Click the gray button at the left edge of the row containing the index name you want to delete, and then press **Delete**. You must delete all the data from all the rows associated with the index name you want to delete. If you don't delete all the information about the index, Access won't let you save the table.

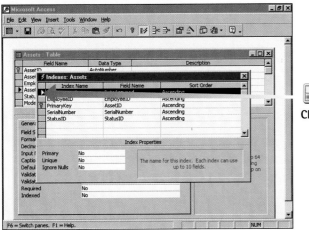

Click

How-To Hints

Don't Panic!

When you delete an index from a field, that's all you delete: the index. You don't delete the field itself, which remains safe and secure with your table.

End

How to Import Data from Another Access Table

When you import data, Access creates a copy of it and inserts it into your table. As you'll notice in the file choices in Step 3, you can import data from Microsoft Excel, a variety of text files, Exchange, Outlook, and Lotus 1-2-3. In this task, we're using the **Our_Inventry** database, which is a renamed version of the **Household Goods** (Inventry.mdb) sample database that comes with Access 2000. We'll be importing data from a Wizard-generated **Asset Tracking** database.

Begin

1 Open the Database Table

Open a database and display the **Database** window. Click **Tables** in the Objects bar and select the table into which you want to import data.

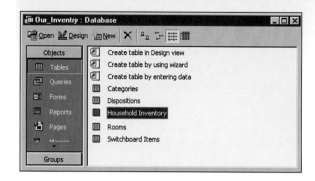

2 Select the Import Command

From the Access menu, select **File, Get External Data, Import**. The **Import** dialog box appears.

3 Set the File Type

Make sure that the **Files of type** option is set to **Microsoft Access**.

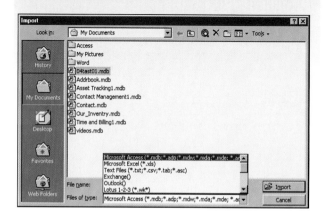

4 Select the Other Database

For this example, select the file Asset Tracking1.mdb, which you've been using throughout this part of the book. (If the file you need is not in the default file path, click the down-arrow to the right of the **Look In** box, and then select the file path and folder for the file from which you want to import data.) Click **Import**.

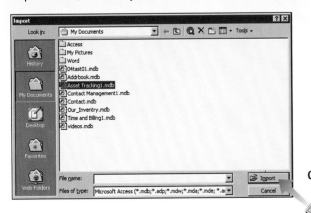

Click

5 Import Objects Box

In the **Import Objects** dialog box, select each table that contains data you want to import. Select multiple tables by holding **Ctrl** as you click the table names. (If you didn't choose to import from an Access file in Step 3, instead of the **Import Objects** dialog box in Step 4, you'll get a wizard to help guide you through the import procedure.) Click **OK**. The selected table or tables now appear in the list of tables for the database.

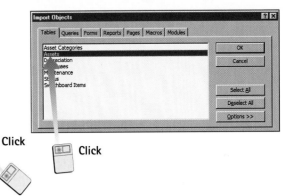

Click

6 The Table Definitions Only Option

If you want to import only the table definitions for the selected fields and not the data itself, click **Options**. In the **Import Tables** area of the expanded dialog box, choose **Definition Only**. Click **OK** to import the data.

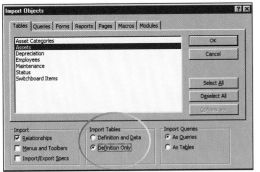

How-To Hints

Here, There, or Anywhere

Remember that if you want changes made to the source file to show up in the other table, and vice versa, you must link the data rather than importing it. A *link* establishes an always updated connection between the tables. You'll learn how to link tables in Project 5.

End

How to Add, Change, and Delete Records

Each horizontal line (row) of information that spans the fields (columns) in a table is called a *record*. You can add, delete, and modify the data in records in a table.

Begin

1 Position the Cursor to Add a Record

Open the database table whose data you want to alter in Datasheet view. Click the **New Record** button at the bottom of the **Table** window to go past the last record in the table to a blank line on which you can enter a new record.

PersonID	Address ID	First Name	Last Name	Nickname	Ro▲
1	1	Paul	Davolio		Spouse
2	1	Daniel	Davolio		Child
3	1	Jean	Davolio		Child
4	2	Anne	Fuller		Spouse
5	2	Paula	Fuller		Child
6	2	John	Fuller		Child
7	2	Helen	Fuller		Child
8	4	Michael	Peacock		Spouse
9	4	Laura	Peacock		Child
10	1	Nancy	Davolio		Contact
11	2	Andrew	Fuller		Contact
12	3	Janet	Leverling		Contact
13	4	Margaret	Peacock		Contact
14	5	Steven	Buchanan		Contact▼

Record: 1 of 15

Click

2 Add a Record

Type data into each field of the table to create a new record. Press **Tab**, use the **right arrow**, or click the field to position the cursor before you type the data. Use the **arrow keys** or the **arrow buttons** at the bottom of the **Table** window to move the cursor from record to record.

PersonID	Address ID	First Name	Last Name	Nickname	Ro▲
4	2	Anne	Fuller		Spouse
5	2	Paula	Fuller		Child
6	2	John	Fuller		Child
7	2	Helen	Fuller		Child
8	4	Michael	Peacock		Spouse
9	4	Laura	Peacock		Child
10	1	Nancy	Davolio		Contact
11	2	Andrew	Fuller		Contact
12	3	Janet	Leverling		Contact
13	4	Margaret	Peacock		Contact
14	5	Steven	Buchanan		Contact
15	5	Steven	Hill		Roomma
(AutoNumber)					

Record: 16 of 16

`Tab⇆`

3 Change a Record

Position the cursor in the field cell that contains data you want to modify. Make the required deletions and type the new information.

Role	Birthdate	Send Card	Date Last Talk	Date Updated	Email A▲
Spouse		No			
Child		No			
Child		No			
Child		No			
Spouse		No			
Child		No			
Contact	08/04/1972	No		1/16/98	
Contact	06/17/1961	No		1/16/98	
Contact	07/14/1965	Yes	12/23/94	1/16/98	
Contact	07/14/1965	Yes		1/16/98	
Contact	08/12/1970	No	11/25/94	1/16/96	
Roommate	01/01/1941	No		5/1/	
		No		5/6/99	

Record: 15 of 15

4 Cross It Out

You can select the entire cell by moving the mouse over the left border of the cell until the pointer changes to a white cross. Click to select the entire cell. When you begin to type, Access completely erases the old information and replaces it with the new data. (If the mouse pointer is not a white cross when you click a cell, you merely position the cursor in the field; you do not select the entire cell.)

Click

5 Cancel Changes

You can cancel the last change you made and return the field to its previous state by pressing the Esc key.

Esc

6 Delete a Record

Move the mouse pointer over the gray button on the left edge of the row containing the record you want to delete. The pointer changes to a black right arrow. Click to select the record. Click the **Delete Record** icon on the **Access** toolbar and click **Yes** when you're prompted to permanently delete the record.

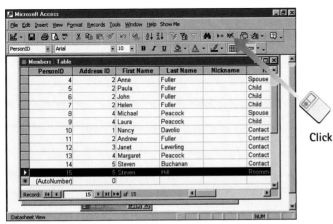

Click

How-To Hints

You Can't Change Your Mind!

Once you've deleted a record, it's gone. So consider carefully before you click **Yes** when Access warns you about deleting the record. If you decide not to delete the record, click **No**.

End

How to Insert and Move a Field

You may have an established table that would be perfect if it had another column to hold some data you didn't plan for when you created the table. Or you may have a table that would be easier to understand if the columns were in a different order. Fortunately, Access lets you manipulate and insert additional fields into an established table.

Begin

1 Insert a Field in Datasheet View

Open the table you want to modify in Datasheet view. Decide where you want the new field, and then click in any row in the field to the right of where you want the new field to appear. For example, if you want the new field to appear between columns 2 and 3, click in column 3.

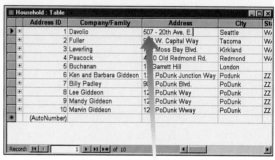

 Click

2 Use the Insert Menu

From the menu bar, select **Insert, Column**. Access inserts the new field with a generic field name. (See Task 3 for information on how to rename the column.)

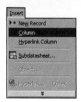

3 Insert a Field in Design View

Click the **View** button on the **Access** toolbar to switch to Design view. Click the name of the field below which you want the new field (row) to appear. (Fields are in rows in Design view.)

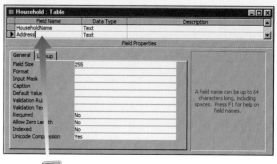

Click

4 Click the Insert Rows Button

On the **Access** toolbar, click the **Insert Rows** button.

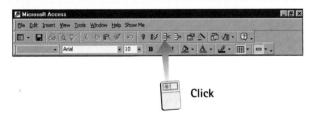

Click

5 Move a Field in Datasheet View

Click the **View** button on the **Access** toolbar to switch to Datasheet view. Select the field you want to move by clicking the field name at the top of the column.

	State/Province	Postal Code	Country	Home Phone	Work Phone	Work E>
+	WA	98122	USA	(504) -9857	(504) 555-9922	
+	WA	98401	USA	(504) 5-9482	(504) 555-9933	
+	WA	98033	USA	(504) 5-3412	(504) 555-9944	
+	WA	98052	USA	(504) 5-8122	(504) 555-9955	
+			UK	(715) 4-848	(715) 555-858	
+	ZZ	00000	USA			
+	ZZ	00000	USA			
+	ZZ	00000	USA			
+	ZZ	00000	USA			
+	ZZ	00000	USA			

Record: 1 of 10

Click

6 Drag and Drop the Field

Drag the column to its new location and release the mouse button.

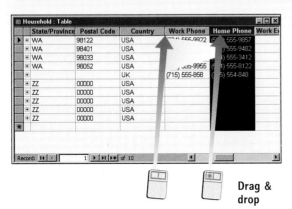

Drag & drop

How-To Hints

Manual All the Way

You cannot undo a column move. If you don't like the new spot, you have to repeat the process and drag it back to its old location.

End

How to Format a Table

Are you at the point where you refer to Access's default text appearance as the "Bill's fault look"? You'll be happy to hear that you don't have to stick with the same old look in all your tables. Changing the font style formatting for a table is easy.

Begin

1 Change the Font Face

Open a table in Datasheet view. Select a column (or press **Ctrl+A** to select the entire table) and pick a new font face from the **Font** drop-down list on the **Formatting** toolbar.

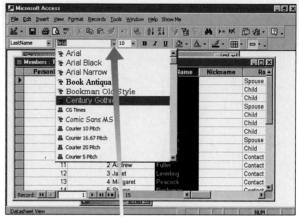

Click

2 Resize the Text

Select any field (for the entire table) and then select a font size from the **Font Size** drop-down list on the **Formatting** toolbar.

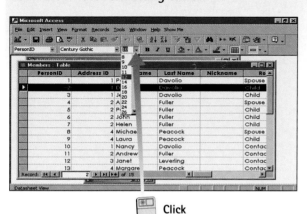

Click

3 Apply a Special Effect

Click the appropriate button on the **Formatting** toolbar to make the text in your table bold, italicized, or underlined. In this case, choose **Bold**.

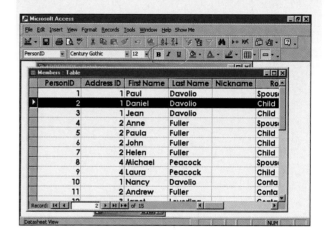

4 Set the Table's Background Color

You can change the table's background color, which is the color behind the text in all the fields. Click the arrow next to the **Fill/Back Color** button on the **Formatting** toolbar and choose a color from the pop-up menu that appears.

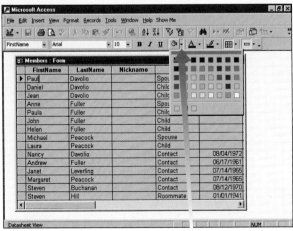

 Click

5 Pick a Different Text Color

You can change the color of the text in the table. Click the arrow next to the **Font/Fore Color** button on the **Formatting** toolbar and choose a color from the pop-up menu.

Click

6 Change the Color of the Grid Lines

To change the color of the grid lines, click the down arrow next to the **Line/Border Color** button on the **Formatting** toolbar and choose a color from the pop-up menu.

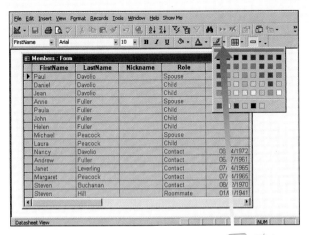

 Click

How-To Hints

Design Considerations

When you pick a new font style, make sure that it is readable both on screen and on paper. Don't go overboard with your changes. Bold and color is best used for emphasis, not to overwhelm.

End

How to Find and Sort Records in a Table

After you've added a large amount of data to your database, it's not practical to search for information by scrolling through the tables. Access makes it easy to do a simple search by using the **Find** button on the **Access** toolbar.

Begin

1 Get Out the Binoculars

Place the cursor in the field you want to search. In this example, you want to search by last name, so position the cursor anywhere in the **Last Name** field. Click the **Find** button (the binoculars) on the toolbar.

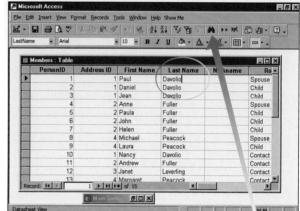

Click

2 Enter the Search Value

In the **Find What** box in the **Find and Replace** dialog box, type a search value (that is, what you are looking for). In this example, you're looking for all records that have the last name *Hill*, so type **Hill**.

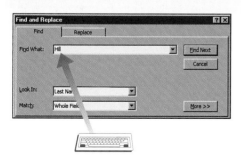

3 Set the Find Options

If it's not already set, select the field you're searching within from the **Look in** pull-down menu. (Because you selected the field before you clicked **Find**, this should already be set.) From the **Match** drop-down list, select an option (**Any Part of Field** is usually the best option).

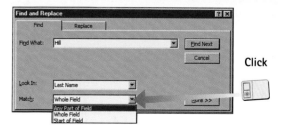
Click

4 Start the Search

Click **Find Next** to begin the records search. If Access finds a matching entry, it selects that entry in the table. If Access finds no matches, it displays a message stating that it was unable to find an item fitting your description.

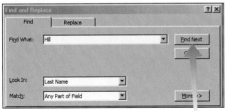

 Click

5 Select a Sort Field

To sort the records in a table, you must first decide which field you want to use to sort them. Click anywhere in the field to position the cursor. In this example, select the **Last Name** field.

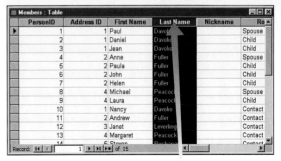

 Click

6 Sort Your Records

Decide whether you want the sort to be ascending (from A to Z) or descending (from Z to A). Click the appropriate button on the toolbar. The records are now sorted in the order you specified.

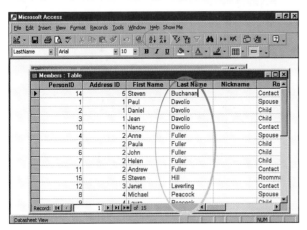

End

How-To Hints

Lookin' for Data in All the Right Places

If you can't remember enough information about the record you are looking for, remember that you can use the **PageUp** and **PageDown** keys on your keyboard to move through the table.

How to Find and Replace Data in a Table

When you have to find and replace large amounts of data or perform calculations on that data, a query works best (see Part 5). However, for simple, one-time search operations, you can find and replace data in a table in Datasheet view. In the **Address Book** database example used in this task, there are several *Davolio* records. Who knew they spelled their last name with an *s* at the end? Although you could scroll through and type the missing *s* several different times, there's an easier way to get the job done.

Begin

1 Start the Replace

To start the replace operation, place the cursor in the field in which you want to perform the search. Select **Edit, Replace** (or press **Ctrl+H**) to bring up the **Find and Replace** dialog box with the **Replace** tab selected.

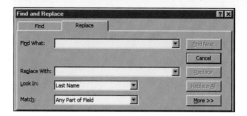

2 Use the Find Button

You can also start the search and replace operation using the **Find** button. Place the cursor in the field in which you want to perform the search. On the toolbar, click the **Find** button (the binoculars) to open the **Find and Replace** dialog box with the **Find** tab selected.

Click

3 Move to the Replace Tab

If it's not already selected, click the **Replace** tab to switch to the "find and replace" portion of the dialog box.

4 Find What

In the **Find What** text box, type the word you want Access to find. In this example, type **Davolio**.

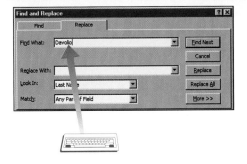

5 Replace With

In the **Replace With** text box, type the word with which you want Access to replace the found word. In this example, type **Davolios**.

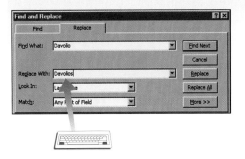

6 Activate the Replace

Click **Replace** if you want to watch Access at work and to make the changes one at a time. Otherwise, click **Replace All**. (When Access is done with the replacing, a dialog box tells you how many words were replaced. Click **OK**.)

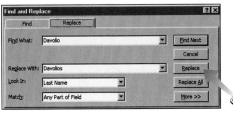

Click

End

How-To Hints

Refine the Search

You can narrow a search by specifying that Access match exact case or display formats. Click the **More** button on the **Find and Replace** dialog box to find these options.

How to Delete a Table from a Database

One of the best ways to keep your databases up-to-date is to delete tables you no longer need. The advantages are smaller database file sizes, less time spent performing routine tasks such as queries, and doing away with clutter. Exercise caution before deleting a working table and its data because once it's gone, it's gone. On the other hand, when you're designing a database, you may find yourself deleting a lot of tables as you update and modify your design.

Begin

1 Close the Table

Before you can delete a table, you must first close it. Click the **Close box** in the upper-right corner of the table window. In this example, you are going to delete the **Role** table from the **Address Book** sample database.

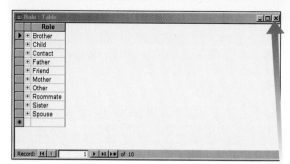

Click

2 Select the Object Type to Delete

In the Objects bar of the **Database** window, click **Tables** if it's not already selected. All the tables in your database appear in the Objects list in the right pane.

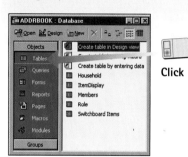

Click

3 Select the Table to Delete

In the Objects list, click the name of the table you want to delete (in this example, the **Role** table has been selected). Make sure that you have selected the correct table.

4 Delete the Table

Press the **Delete** key on your keyboard. Access asks whether you're sure you want to delete the table. Double-check to make sure that you really want to delete that table.

Del

5 Confirm the Deletion

Click **Yes** if you do indeed want to delete the indicated table. If you want to back out, click **No**.

Click

6 Delete Any Table Relationships

If the table you are trying to delete has *relationships* to other tables, you must delete those relationships first. (See Task 5 in this part to learn more about relationships.) The **Role** table has relationships to other tables, so click **Yes** at the **Do you want Microsoft Access to delete the relationships now?** prompt. (If you choose **No** at this prompt, the table is not deleted.)

Click

End

How-To Hints

Delete Other Objects

To delete an object other than a table, simply select that object type from the Objects bar in the **Database** window. For example, in Step 2, click **Queries, Forms, Reports, Pages, Macros,** or **Modules** and then continue. The dialog boxes may be a little different depending on the object type you've selected, but the basic process is the same.

Stop the Warning Box

Although it isn't recommended, you can click the **Help** button on the warning dialog box if you want to prevent a warning box from appearing every time you attempt to delete an object.

17

How to Open and Use the Performance Analyzer

You can optimize the performance of your Access databases, or individual objects within them, by using the Access Performance Analyzer. The Analyzer doesn't look at the performance of Access or of your computer system; instead, it goes over the components that make up your databases. When you run the Analyzer, you are given three types of analysis results: Recommendation, Suggestion, and Idea. Access performs the Recommendation and Suggestion optimizations if you choose to do them. However, you have to do the Idea optimizations on your own.

Begin

1 Open the Database

From the **Access** menu bar, choose **File**, **Open** to display the **Open** dialog box. Select the database file you want to analyze by double-clicking it.

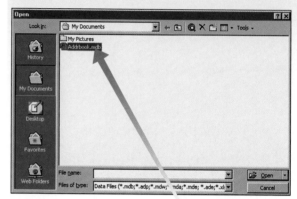

Double-click

2 Open the Performance Analyzer

Select **Tools, Analyze, Performance** to display the **Performance Analyzer** dialog box.

3 Select Database Objects

Make sure that the **Tables** tab is in the foreground. Select the database tables you want the Performance Analyzer to check by clicking the box next to each object. Alternatively, click **Select All** to select all the objects listed on that tab.

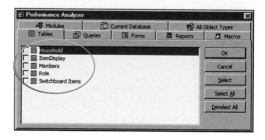

4 Start the Analyzer

When you have selected all the database objects you want to analyze, click **OK** to start the Performance Analyzer. (Note that you can switch to other tabs and select queries, forms, and reports to optimize as well as tables.)

Click

5 View the Results

The Performance Analyzer returns up to three kinds of results: Recommendations, Suggestions, and Ideas. If your database was particularly well designed, you'll see a dialog box stating that the Performance Analyzer has no suggestions to improve the objects you selected.

End

How-To Hints

What Performance Analyzer Works On

The Access Performance Analyzer checks optimization possibilities for your tables, queries, forms, reports, macros, and modules of your Access *databases.* (It does not analyze Access *projects,* which are beyond the scope of this book.)

If you need to perform an optimization, choose one or more of the items in the **Analysis Results** list. Information about optimizing each item can be viewed in the **Analysis Notes** box. To proceed with optimizing any of the analysis results items, select an item (or click the **Select All** button) and then click the **Optimize** button. Access performs the optimizations you selected. If you agree with an Idea's results, you must perform that optimization on your own, following the suggestions Access provides.

For help with optimizing Access projects, ask the Office Assistant for help or select the **Help** menu option.

Project 2

Exploring Access Database Wizards

By now, you may have noticed that a database is nothing more than...*drum roll, please*...a collection of data. Yep. That's all there is to it. Well, not completely. But that's enough info to get you started on Project 2.

You probably use databases extensively already and are not even aware of it. Your birthday card list is a database. You use another database every time you look something up in the phone book. And, whether it's balanced or not, your checkbook is also a database. These are known as "flat file" databases because, even though the balance in your checkbook may directly relate to how much money you can afford to stick inside that next birthday card on your list, the two lists aren't linked in a *relational* sort of way. You'll understand what this means as you work through this project and the others in this book.

Chances are that all of the databases generated by the Access 2000 Database Wizard are too complex for your needs at this stage. But don't let that deter you. We strongly believe it helps to first see the goal you want to attain and then to step back and learn the steps necessary to reach that goal. That's how this project can help.

1 Open Access

From the **Start** menu, choose **Programs, Microsoft Access**. (If Access is already open on your system, choose **New** from the Database toolbar choose the **Databases** tab, and then skip to Step 3.)

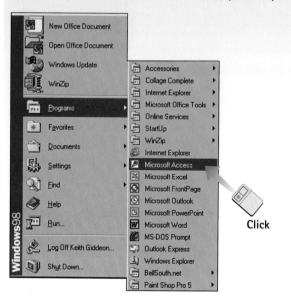

Click

2 Start the Wizard

When the Microsoft Access **Startup** dialog box appears, choose **Access database wizards, pages, and projects**. Click **OK**.

3 Choose a Database

In the **New** dialog box, click the **Databases** tab. Choose **Contact Management** and then click **OK**.

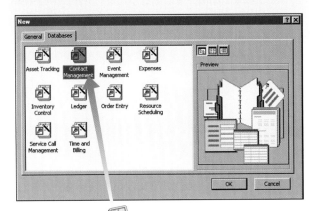

Click

5 Database Wizard Dialog Box

Your **Project2: Database** window appears in the Access window while the wizard opens. The first **Database Wizard** dialog box advises you that the Contact Management database will store contact information and call information. Click **Next**.

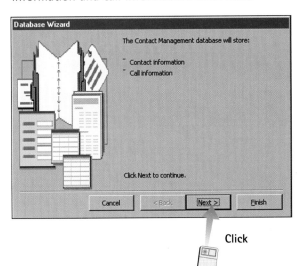

Click

4 Assign a Filename

The wizard opens the **File New Database** dialog box to the **My Documents** folder. Because you want to store your database files in a new folder, click the **Create New Folder** button on the dialog box's toolbar. When prompted, type the new folder name **Test**. In the **File name** box back in the **File New Database** dialog box, type the filename **Project2**. Microsoft Access adds the .MDB file extension automatically. Click **Create**.

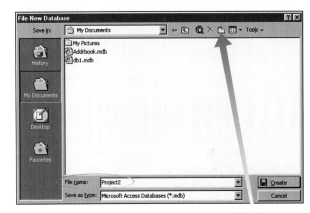

Click

How-To Hints

Installing the Wizard

If this is the first time you've run the Database Wizard, you may see a dialog box telling you that the wizard isn't part of the standard installation. Put your Office 2000 CD-ROM in the drive and click **Yes** to install the wizard.

If You Want Reports

You must have a printer installed if you want the wizard to complete the Report portion of a new database setup.

Continues

6 View Required Fields

In the left pane, the Database Wizard shows the three tables in your **Project2** database. The right pane shows the fields for the selected table. Click one of the fields that has a check mark to deselect that field. Odds are that if the field is checked, you'll see a dialog box warning you that the field is required.

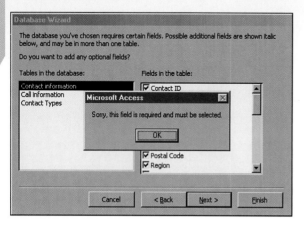

7 Activate Optional Fields

In the left pane, select **Contact information**. In the right pane, scroll down to view some optional fields (those without check marks). Click the empty box next to a field to include that field in the database you are building. In the left pane, click **Call information** and **Contact types** to see the fields in these tables. Click **Next**.

Selected fields

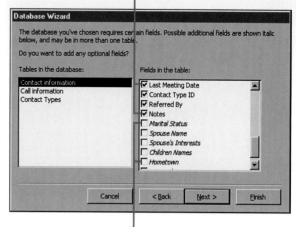

Optional fields

8 Preview Screen Display Styles

To preview a screen display style, click the style name in the right pane. You'll see the selected background in the lower-left pane.

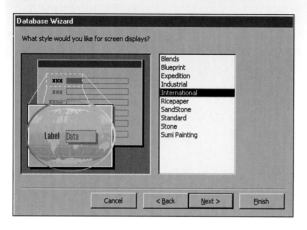

9 Select a Screen Display Style

For the sample database, select the **Blends** style. After you make your selection, click **Next**.

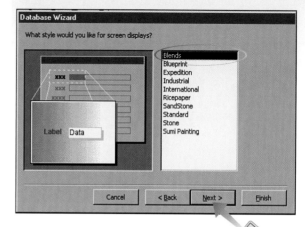

Click

10 Preview the Printed Report Styles

Now you're faced with a decision about which font style you prefer for printed reports. Select styles from the right pane and view the results in the left pane.

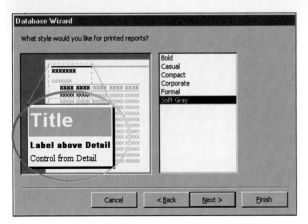

11 Select a Printed Reports Style

For the sample database, select the **Bold** style. Click **Next**.

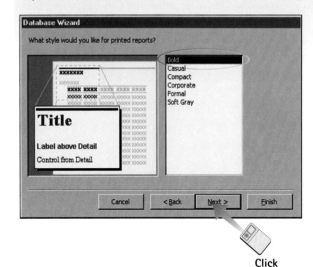

Click

12 Name Your Database

Type the name you want to give your database. (This name is different than the filename you entered in Step 4.) In this case, type **Contact Management**. Click Next.

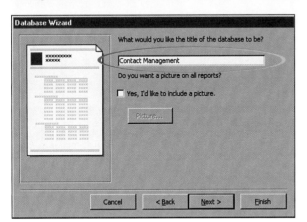

Continues

How-To Hints

You Can Go Back

If you change your mind while you're still in the wizard, you can click **Back** instead of **Next**. If what appears onscreen isn't to your liking (as far as font style and so on) and you haven't yet begun to enter data, you can always delete the database and run the wizard again. Otherwise, you can make changes later, as explained in Part 4, "Creating and Working with Access Tables," and in Part 6, "Creating and Working with Access Forms."

13 The Final Step

The Database Wizard is now ready to create your database based on the information you've entered. Click **Finish** if you're ready to proceed.

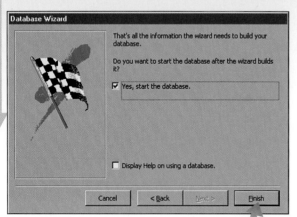

Click

14 The Main Switchboard

After the Database Wizard has created your database, it opens it to the **Main Switchboard**. We'll discuss this form more starting with Step 20.

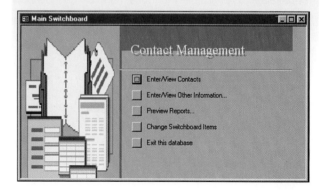

15 View Table Relationships

To use data in one table with corresponding records in another table, Access 2000 must be able to *relate* the tables. To see the relationships between the tables in the database you just created, choose **Tools, Relationships** from the menu bar. Close the dialog box when you are done.

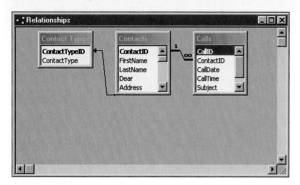

How-To Hints

Kinda Like Kissin' Cousins

In Part 4, Task 5, "How to Establish Table Relationships," you'll learn more about establishing relationships between tables by relating common fields (fields with common values). For now, suffice it to say that the more boxes there are in the Relationships dialog box with lines going between them, the more complex the database relationships.

16 Create More Samples

Choose **Exit this database** from the **Main Switchboard**. To view the relationships in some other databases, run the wizard again. Do so now by clicking **New** on the toolbar, selecting the **Databases** tab, and selecting a new wizard. When you get to the wizard's **Finish** screen, select the **Display Help on using a database** option and click **Finish**.

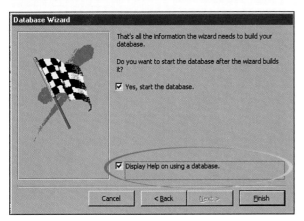

17 Display Help Automatically

If you followed the **Finish** screen's instructions in Step 16, you'll see the Access 2000 Help file called **Work with a database**. Clippit, the Office Assistant, is there too. Click one of the Help topics if you want to read more at this time.

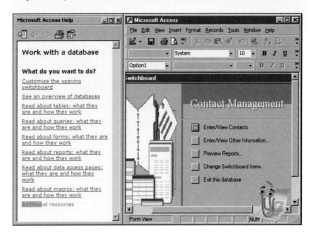

18 View Asset Tracking Relationships

To view the relationships (or links) between the tables in the sample database you just created, click the **Main Switchboard** to bring it forward. From the **Tools** menu, select **Relationships**. The relationships shown here span six tables in the **Asset Tracking** database; the database you created may have more or fewer relationships.

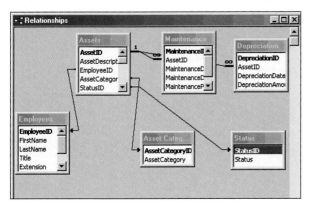

Continues

How-To Hints

You May Need More Information

Before the Database Wizard can finish creating the database you selected in Step 16, you may have to enter your company name, address, and so on. Enter the appropriate information and click the **Close box** (the X in the upper-right corner of the dialog box's title bar). Then the wizard will display the Main Switchboard and Help screens.

The Office Assistant you see on your screen may not be Clippit, and you may not even see an Assistant. For information about displaying the Assistant and selecting a different character, refer to Part 2, "Finding Help with Access."

19 Time and Billing Relationships

Look at the 10 tables in the **Time and Billing** database shown here. You don't have to create this sample database—just look at the figure here. Notice how these tables relate to one another. (You may have to scroll to the right to see them all.)

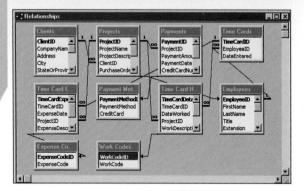

20 Entering Contact Data

If you closed the **Project2** database earlier, reopen it at this time by selecting **File, Open** from the menu bar. From the **Main Switchboard**, click **Enter/View Contacts**. Name and address information goes on **Page: 1**; enter information for a hypothetical contact now, pressing Tab or Enter between fields. You can read more about data entry in Part 3, Task 5, "How to Use the Switchboard to Access Objects."

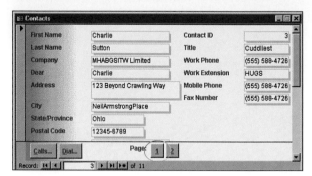

21 Enter Contact Types on Page: 2

Click the **Page: 2** icon at the bottom of the **Contacts** screen. You can add entries to the **Contact Type** field's drop-down list (which will be helpful as you continue to add contacts to the database). To add contact types to the list, double-click the **Contact Type** field and enter the contact types. Click the **Close box** to close the dialog box when you are done. Then click the drop-down arrow to see your list and select an entry.

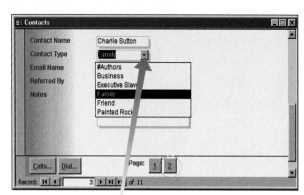

Double-click

How-To Hints

Understanding Relationships

A *relationship* is an association that's based on some common data in two fields (columns) in a database. Access 2000 relationships can be of the following varieties:

✓ **One-to-one.** There is only one record in each table that links the tables. For example, in the **Project2** database, only the **ContactID** field links the **Contacts** and **Calls** tables.

✓ **One-to-many.** The linking value in one table links to more than one record in the other table, but a record in the second table can have only one matching record in the first table.

✓ **Many-to-many.** The linking values appear in numerous records in both tables.

22 Alphabetical Contact Listing

After you've entered some contacts, close the **Contacts** window by clicking the **Close button** in the title bar. From the **Main Switchboard**, click **Preview Reports**. Choose **Preview the Alphabetical Contact Listing Report**. Notice that the contacts you entered in Step 21 appear on this report.

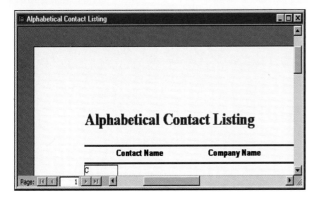

23 View the Report Onscreen

Your monitor size and screen resolution will determine the optimal settings for your report. Select **75%** from the **Zoom** control's drop-down list in the toolbar, and maximize the report screen to see whether you like that onscreen image. Or else right-click anywhere in the report and select **Zoom: Fit**.

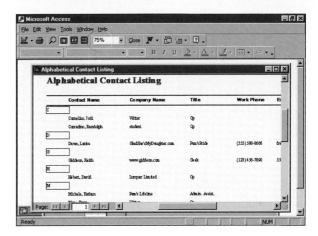

24 Export the Report to Word

For those times when you want to save an RTF (rich text format) file to print later, you can export the report to Microsoft Word and print it from there. From the **Tools** menu, select **Office Links, Publish It with MS Word**. (Alternatively, click the Office Links button in the toolbar.) Access 2000 automatically displays your report in Word and saves it as an RTF file. Exit Word and return to Access 2000.

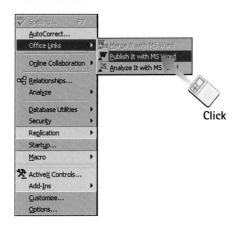

Click

25 Exit the Database

In Access 2000, exit the **Alphabetical Contact Listing Report** (click the **Close button** in the report's title bar). Continue to explore your other options by returning to the **Main Switchboard**. Click **Exit this database** when you're ready to quit.

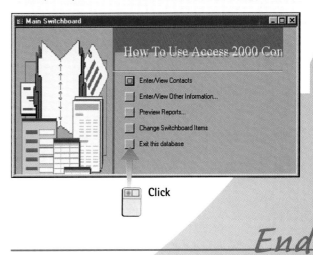

Click

End

Task

5

Working with Database Table Queries

A query gathers data from fields you specify in one or more tables in your database. You will find queries useful for gathering data from several tables, especially if that data changes on a regular basis. The time you save by using queries, instead of manually entering data into a new table—and updating the data in the new table, can be great. The query returns the data in Datasheet view. These results are called a *query set*.

In Part 5, you'll learn how to create a number of different queries, as well as how to perform calculations within those queries. ●

How to Create a Select Query

The most common type of query is called a *select query*. A select query returns a result set, or list of records, based upon a question asked about the data contained in tables. In this task, you'll use the **Address Book** sample database and query it to view only the information you want to see: the names of the people in your address book and their email addresses.

We've added three email addresses in the Members table for this task. Add some email addresses to this table before starting this task.

Begin

1 Show the Query Objects

With the **Address Book** database open to the **Database** window, click the **Queries** button on the Objects bar to show the list of objects in queries.

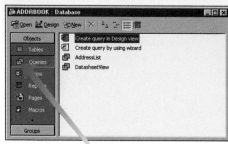

Click

2 Open a New Query

On the **Database** window toolbar, click **New** to open the **New Query** dialog box.

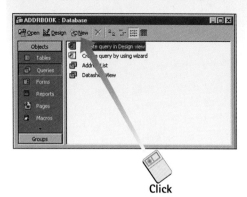

Click

3 Start the Simple Query Wizard

From the list in the right pane of the **New Query** dialog box, select **Simple Query Wizard**. (A *simple query* is a type of select query.) Click **OK**.

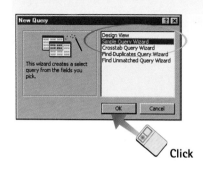

Click

4 Select the Query Fields

From the **Tables/Queries** list in the wizard dialog box, select the table from which you want to choose fields for your new query (**Table: Members**). From the **Available Fields** pane, select the fields from which you want to retrieve data (**FirstName, LastName,** and **EmailAddress**). If you want, select another table and its related fields until all the fields you want to query are listed in the **Selected Fields** pane. Click **Next**.

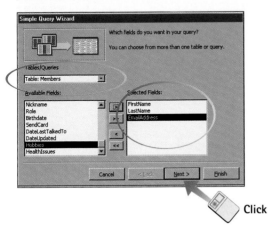

Click

5 Name the Query

Type a name for your new query. Select the **Open the query to view information** radio button. If you wish, click the **Display Help on working with the query?** checkbox. Click **Finish**.

6 View the Query

The new query appears in Datasheet view. To open this query at a later time, choose the name of the query from the **Queries Object** list.

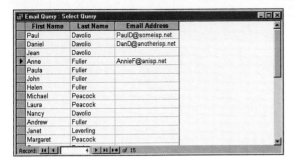

End

How-To Hints

Going Fishing

Because a relational database uses storage space economically, data can reside in a number of different tables. Although such a storage scheme eliminates redundancy, it doesn't make it easy for you to see a broad range of your data at once. However, if you bait your hook (establish your query criteria), cast your line (run the query), and land your catch (move your query data into a display format), you can see just the records and fields you want to see.

How to Create a Make-Table Query

A make-table query is an **action query** (makes changes to data) which creates a new table in the database from data in one or more tables. This task uses the **Employees** table in the **Northwind** sample database. You want to query the table so that you can view only those persons hired after June 1, 1993. To do this, you'll create a make-table query derived from a simple query.

Begin

1 Show the Query Objects

With the **Northwind** sample database, usually found in the \Microsoft Office\Office\Samples folder, open to the **Database** window, click the **Queries** button on the Objects bar to show the list of objects in queries.

Click

2 Open a New Simple Query

On the **Database** window toolbar, click New to open the New Query dialog box.

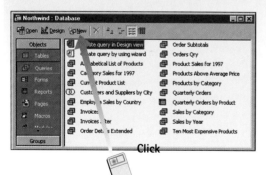
Click

3 Start the Simple Query Wizard

From the list in the right pane of the New Query dialog box, select **Simple Query Wizard** and click **OK**.

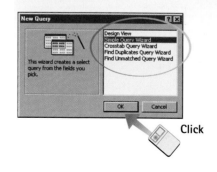
Click

4 Select the Query Fields

From the **Tables/Queries** list in the wizard dialog box, select the table from which you want to choose fields for your new query (**Table: Employees**). From the **Available Fields** pane, select the fields from which you want to retrieve data (**FirstName, LastName,** and **HireDate**). Click **Next**.

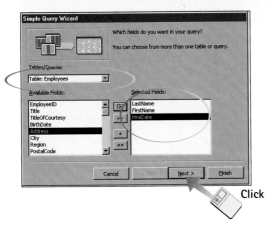

Click

5 Name the Query

Type a name for your new query. Select the radio button next to **Modify the query design** and click **Finish**.

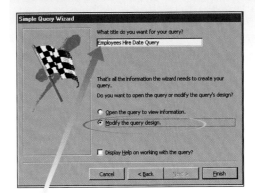

6 Start the Make-Table Query

The new simple query opens in Design view. Click the arrow next to the **Query Type** button on the **Access** toolbar and select **Make-Table Query** (you may have to expand the menu to locate this option).

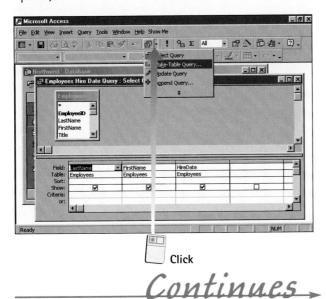

Click

Continues

How-To Hints

The Difference Between Select and Make-Table Queries

A select query simply returns a result set based on a question asked about the data. A make-table query creates a new table for a database by copying records from existing tables.

How to Create a Make-Table Query Continued

7 Name the Table

In the **Make Table** dialog box, type the name you want for the new table that will be created.

8 Add to Current Database

Click the **Current Database** radio button to add the new table to the **Northwind** sample database. Click **OK**.

Click

9 Add Fields to the Query Design

If you decide you want more fields than you originally selected, drag the additional field names from the **Employees** field list in the upper half of the window to a blank **Field** cell in the design grid in the lower half of the window. This action isn't necessary in this example because you want just the three fields.

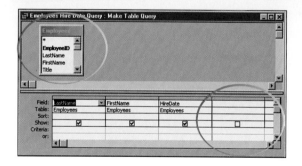

10 Set the Query Criteria

Because you want a table that contains only those employees hired after June 1993, add criteria to the query. In the **Criteria** cell for the **HireDate** field, type Between #06/01/93# And #07/31/99#. (Use some other future date if you will be using this new table more than once.)

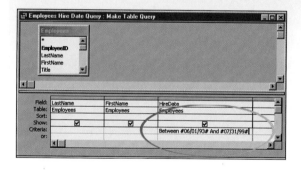

11 Preview the New Table

When you have added all the necessary information to the design grid for the new table, it's time to preview it. Click the **View** button in the toolbar to see the results in Datasheet view. Click **View** again to return to Design view if you want to make changes or are ready to run (running a query saves it to the database) the query.

Click

12 Run the Query

Create the new table by clicking the **Run** toolbar button (the large red exclamation point). If you get a warning message asking whether you want to paste rows into the new table, click **Yes**. To view the results of the query, open the table from the **Database** window.

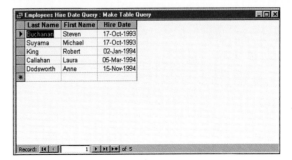

End

How-To Hints

Delete a Field from a Query

You can delete a field from your query, but you must do so before you run the query. You can't alter the results of a query. To delete a field, simply select that field in the query design grid (in Design view) and press the Delete key. To delete more than one field from your query, hold down the Ctrl key as you select the fields. The deletions you make from the query do not affect the actual tables from which the chosen fields are taken. After making your changes, click the **Run** button on the toolbar to process the query.

More on Query Criteria Expressions

To learn more about criteria expressions, go to the Contents tab in Access Help. Find the Using Criteria and Expressions to Retrieve Data folder within the Working with Queries folder.

How to Create an Update Query

An *update query* is useful when you want to change data that duplicates other records or fields. The update query can make changes faster than a find and replace operation (discussed in Task 15 of Part 4, "Creating and Working with Access Tables"). In this task, you'll continue to use the **Northwind** sample database. You've noticed that the unit price of the Chai product has increased from $18.00 to $20.25. Although several other products have the same unit price as the Chai, you want to change the unit price for only the Chai product.

Begin

1 Show the Query Objects

With the **Northwind** sample database open to the **Database** window, click the **Queries** button on the Objects bar to show the list of objects in queries.

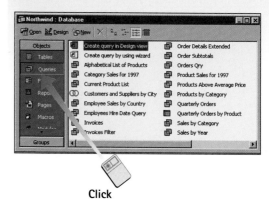

Click

2 Open a New Simple Query

On the **Database** window toolbar, click **New** to open the **New Query** dialog box.

Click

3 Start the Simple Query Wizard

From the list in the right pane of the **New Query** dialog box, select **Simple Query Wizard** and click **OK**.

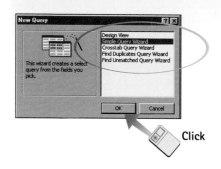

Click

4 Select the Query Fields

From the **Tables/Queries** list in the wizard dialog box, select the table from which you want to choose fields for your new query (**Table: Products**). From the **Available Fields** pane, select the fields from which you want to retrieve data (**ProductName** and **UnitPrice**). Click **Next**.

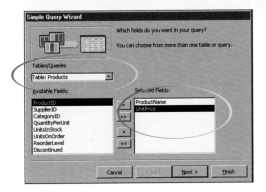

5 Name the Query

When you're asked whether you want a detail or a summary query, select **Details** and click **Next**. In the text box on the next wizard pane, type a name for the new query. Select the **Modify the query design** radio button and click **Finish**.

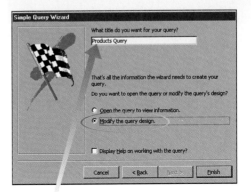

6 Start the Update Query

The new simple query opens in Design view. Click the arrow next to the **Query Type** button on the toolbar and select **Update Query**.

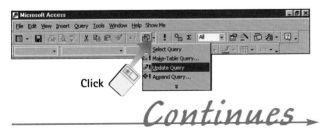

Click

Continues

How-To Hints

Print Your Results

When you print your query results, the printout looks like the results in Datasheet view. To preview the printout results, choose **File, Print Preview** from the **Access** menu. To print the results immediately, click the **Print** button on the **Access** toolbar. Making a printout of your query results is sometimes quicker than creating a report (see Part 7, "Creating Access Reports").

7 Add Fields to the Query Design

If you decide you want more fields than you originally selected, drag the additional field names from the **Products** field list in the upper half of the window to a blank **Field** cell in the design grid in the lower half of the window. This action isn't necessary in this example because you want just the two fields.

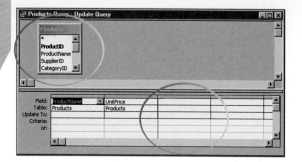

8 Set the Product Criteria

In the **Criteria** cell for the **Products** field, type Chai to limit the update to just the Chai record. (Notice that quotation marks appear around the word you've typed when you move the cursor out of the cell.)

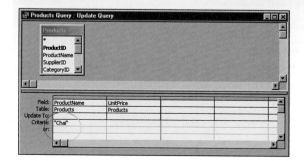

9 Set the Unit Price Criteria

In the **Criteria** cell for the **UnitPrice** field, type 18.00. By entering this value, you are telling the query to search for 18.00 in the Chai record's **UnitPrice** field.

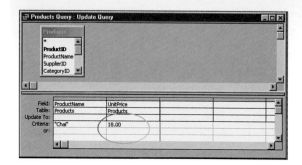

10 Set the Update Data

In the **Update To** cell for the **UnitPrice** field, type 20.25 (the new unit price for the product Chai). Notice that the value **18.00** has changed to **18** in the **Criteria** cell for **UnitPrice**.

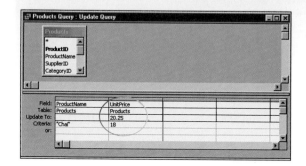

11 Preview Record Changes

When you have added all the information for the update, preview it. Click the **View** button on the toolbar to switch to Datasheet view. The new unit price for the Chai record does not appear. Click **View** again to switch back to Design view so that you can make changes or run the query.

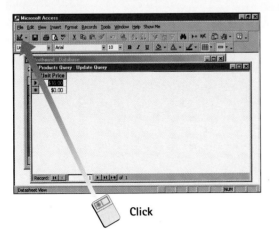

Click

12 Run the Query

In Design view, click the **Run** button on the toolbar (the red exclamation mark). If you receive a message warning that you are about to update the records, click **Yes**. Close the query window, choosing **Yes** when prompted to save the query. When you open the **Products** table from the **Database** window, notice the changes.

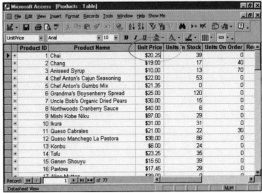

End

How-To Hints

Quotation Marks in the Criteria Cell

When you enter the limiting information in the Design view's **Criteria** cell, you don't have to type the quotation marks around the criteria. Access does that for you automatically, if it applies to the type of expression you've entered.

Limit Results Based on a Field's First Letter

If you want to limit a query's results from a field to names beginning with the letters N-Z, enter the following expression in the Criteria field: >="N". For letters beginning with A-N, enter: <="N".

How to Create a Delete Query

A *delete query* is useful if you want to remove records from a table. This is especially helpful if you have old data that is no longer of any use to you or that is archived.

This task continues the use of the **Northwind** sample database. In this task, you want to delete all records of orders more than one year old. Because each order record has a date field, this process will be relatively easy.

Begin

1 Show the Query Objects

With the **Northwind** sample database open to the **Database** window, click the **Queries** button on the **Objects** bar to show the list of objects in queries.

Click

2 Open a New Simple Query

On the **Database** window toolbar, click **New** to open the **New Query** dialog box.

Click

3 Start the Simple Query Wizard

From the list in the right pane of the **New Query** dialog box, select **Simple Query Wizard** and click **OK**.

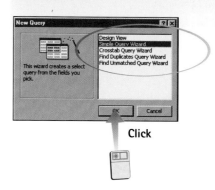
Click

4 Select the Query Fields

From the **Tables/Queries** list in the wizard dialog box, select the table from which you want to choose fields for your new query (**Table: Orders**). From the **Available Fields** pane, select the fields from which you want to retrieve data (**OrderDate** and **ShipName**). Click **Next**.

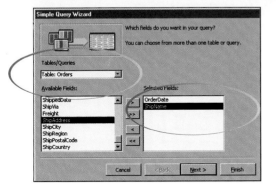

5 Name the Query

In the text box on the next wizard pane, type a name for the new query. Select the **Modify the query design** radio button and click **Finish**.

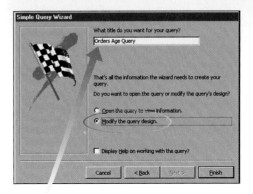

6 Start the Delete Query

The new simple query opens in Design view. Click the arrow next to the **Query Type** button on the toolbar and select **Delete Query**. (Note that you may have to expand the menu to see this option.)

Click

Continues

How-To Hints

Use Caution When Deleting Records

Make sure that you've thought through which records you want to delete. A delete query cannot be undone after it is run.

Therefore...

Back up your tables, by copying them, before you run a delete query. The delete query is irreversible, so you can't go home again—unless the data is preserved in a safe backup copy of the tables. Once you run the query, and all is fine with the results, you can then delete your backup copies of the tables.

.

.

.

.

How to Create a Delete Query Cont.

7 Set the Criteria

In the **Criteria** cell for the **OrderDate** field, type <Date()-365. This formula tells the query to search for and delete records older than 365 days (one year).

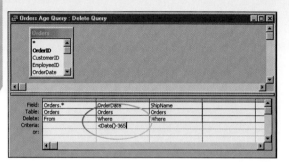

8 Preview Record Deletions

Click **View** on the toolbar to preview the records that will be deleted based on the criteria you just specified. In this example, *all* the records are for orders older than a year, so all the records have been selected for deletion.

9 Return to Design View

When you're through previewing those records to be deleted, click the **View** button on the toolbar again to return to Design view.

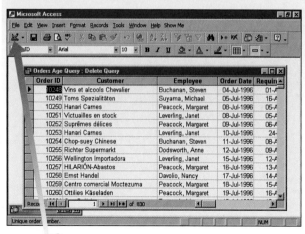

Click

10 Run the Query

In Design view, click the **Run** button on the toolbar to run the query and actually delete the records you saw listed in Step 9.

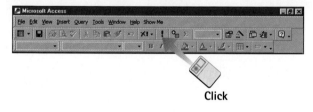

Click

11 Confirm Record Deletions

Access asks whether you're sure you want to delete the number of records affected by your query. Click **Yes** if you're sure. Access changes the **Orders** table. To view the changed table, open it from the **Tables Objects** list in the **Database** window.

Click

End

How-To Hints

Sort a Query

You can sort a query's results by any field you choose. In Design view, choose **Ascending** or **Descending** in the **Sort** cell for the field (column) by which you want to sort.

Multiple Fields Sort Reminder

Remember that Access sorts fields in left-to-right order. For example, if you want to sort by last name and then by first name, the **LastName** field must be to the *left* of the **FirstName** field in the table. See Task 12 of Part 4 for information on how to move fields in Datasheet view.

How to Create a Crosstab Query

A **crosstab query** usually uses an existing query and summarizes data by performing calculations on groups of data. For the most part, a crosstab query categorizes data facts, or groups of data. For instance, if you want to view the monthly orders for a particular product for a portion of your customers or for all of them, a crosstab query is your best choice.

In this task, you'll continue to work with the **Northwind** database. This time, you'll use the supplied **Orders Qry** to see all orders generated by one employee.

Begin

1 Start the Query

With the **Northwind** sample database open to the **Database** window, click the **Queries** button on the **Objects** bar to show the list of objects in queries. On the **Database** window toolbar, click **New** to open the **New Query** dialog box.

 Click

2 Select the Query Wizard

From the list in the right pane of the **New Query** dialog box, select **Crosstab Query Wizard** and click **OK**.

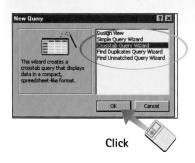

Click

3 Select a Query

In the first pane of the wizard, look at the **View** options under the list box. Select **Queries**. Scroll through the list of queries and tables available in the current database and choose **Orders Qry**. (Because this is a sample database, the query already exists.) Click **Next**.

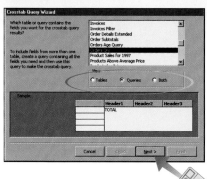

Click

4 Select the Row Headings

Select the fields you want to use as row headings in the result set. You can choose up to three fields. In this example, choose **ShipCountry**. Click **Next**.

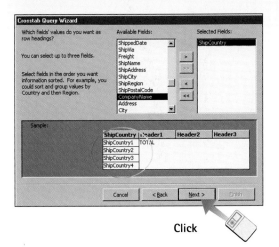

Click

5 Choose Column Headings

Select the single field you want to use as a column heading. In this example, you want to know the freight costs per country and company, so choose **CompanyName**. Click **Next**.

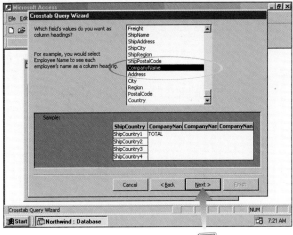

Click

6 Choose Summary Options

Access asks you to define the calculation you want to take place in the result set. From the **Functions** list, select **Sum**. From the **Fields** list, select the field whose values you want to count (in this example, select **Freight**). Click the check box next to **Yes, include row sums** and then click **Next**.

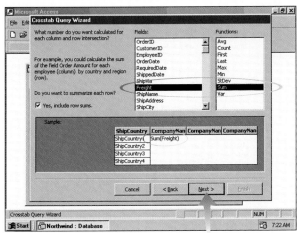

Click

Continues

How-To Hints

Crosstab Query Caution

Unlike many of the other query types, a crosstab query isn't as reusable because it bases its results on *items* in a field. If those items change, data is left out of the query results because the structure of the crosstab query itself isn't updated.

7 Name the Query

In the text box on the next wizard pane, type a name for the new query. Select the **Modify the design** radio button and click **Finish**. The query appears in Design view.

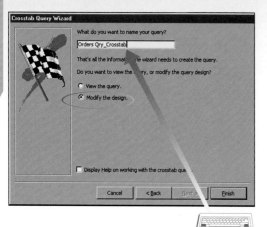

8 Set the Criteria

In the **Criteria** cell for the **ShipCountry** field, type **"Germany"**. This entry tells the query to search for records matching those of the **ShipCountry** named "Germany".

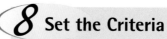
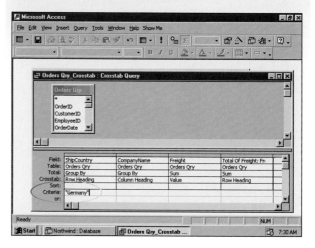

9 Preview the Query Records

Click the **View** button on the toolbar to preview the records selected by the query options you have specified.

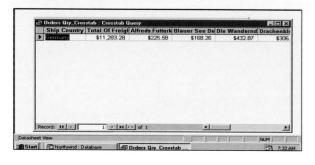

10 Return to Design View

When you're through previewing the records, click the **View** button on the toolbar again to return to Design view.

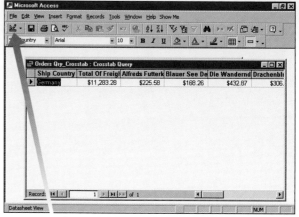

 Click

11 Run the Query

In Design view, click the **Run** button on the toolbar to run the query.

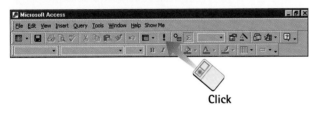

Click

12 View and Save the Query

When you're done working with the query, click the **Close box** in the upper-right corner of the query window. Access prompts you to save the query. If you want to save the query, click **Yes**.

Click

End

How-To Hints

Get Fancy

You can include more than one table in a crosstab query, but doing so requires some fancy footwork first. Use the Simple Query Wizard to create a select query that includes all the fields you need. Then base your crosstab query using that select query instead of on a table. In Step 3 of this task, instead of selecting a single table, you selected an existing query that does just as described here.

How to Print Query Data

At times, you will want to see a query's result set printed out on paper. The result set is shown in Datasheet view, which looks just like a table does in Datasheet view. In this task, you'll print the query result set of the query you created in Task 5.

Begin

1 Open the Queries Object List

With the **Northwind** sample database open to the **Database** window, click the **Queries** button on the Objects bar to show the list of objects in queries.

 Click

2 Open the Query

Select the query whose result set you want to print. For this example, select **Orders Qry_Crosstab** (the name of the query created in Task 5) and click **Open**.

 Click

3 Select Records

If you want to print all the records contained in the query result set, simply click the **Print** button on the **Query Datasheet** toolbar.

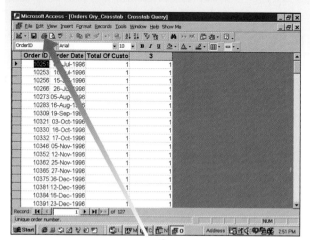

 Click

4 Open the Print Dialog Box

If you want to print only some of the records from the result set, drag over the records to select those you want to print. Then choose **File, Print** to open the **Print** dialog box.

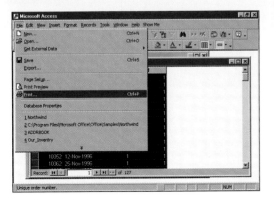

5 Select the Print Range

Select the **Selected Records(s)** option in the **Print Range** area of the **Print** dialog box. You can also specify how many copies of the printout you want by adjusting the value in the **Number of Copies** field.

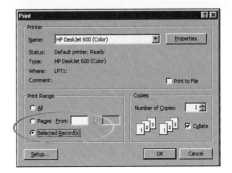

6 Start Printing

Click **OK** to print the selected records.

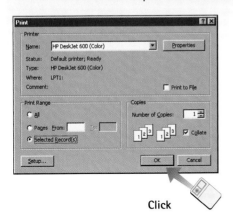

Click

End

How-To Hints

Preview the Datasheet

Before you print from a datasheet, you can preview it by clicking the **Print Preview** button on the toolbar or by choosing **File, Print Preview** from the menu bar.

Sorting Records

If you want to sort the records in a datasheet for your printout, click the gray field name bar for the field you want to use to sort the records. This selects the entire column. Click either the **Sort Ascending** or **Sort Descending** button on the toolbar.

How to Perform Calculations

Formulas allow you to add, subtract, multiply, divide, and do other things to two fields within a query. The result of the formula is displayed in a third column of the query. In this task, you'll continue to use the **Northwind** sample database. You'll use the **Order Details** table, which contains the fields **UnitPrice** and **Quantity**. You want to add a field that calculates the total price (**UnitPrice * Quantity**).

Begin

1 Show the Query Objects

With the **Northwind** sample database open to the **Database** window, click the **Queries** button on the Objects bar to show the list of objects in queries.

Click

2 Open a New Simple Query

On the **Database** window toolbar, click New to open the **New Query** dialog box.

Click

3 Start the Simple Query Wizard

Select **Simple Query Wizard** from the list on the right side of the **New Query** dialog box and click **OK**.

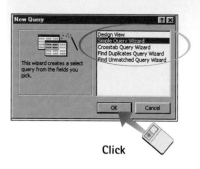

Click

4 Select the Query Fields

From the **Tables/Queries** list in the wizard dialog box, select the table from which you want to choose fields for your new query (**Table: Order Details**). From the **Available Fields** pane, select the fields from which you want to retrieve data (click the >> button to select all the fields). Click **Next**.

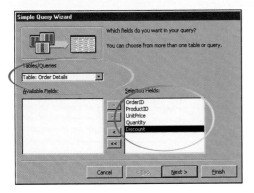

5 Name the Query

When you're asked whether you want a detailed or a summary query, select **Detail (shows every field of every record)** and click **Next**. In the text box on the next wizard pane, type a name for this new query. Select the **Modify the query design** option and click **Finish**.

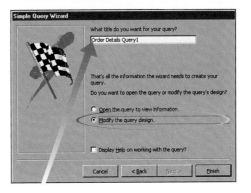

6 Enter the Expression

In the bottom pane, scroll right until you come to an open **Field** cell in which you can enter a name. Type the expression TotalPrice: [UnitPrice]*[Quantity]. This expression tells Access that the **TotalPrice** field equals the **UnitPrice** field multiplied by the **Quantity** field.

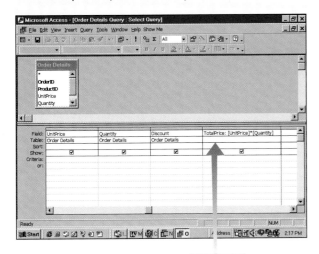

How-To Hints

What the Totals Button Does

You can toggle this button (located on the Database toolbar), in Design view, to display or hide the Total row in the design grid for a select, crosstab, make-table, or append query. This allows you to group data in the open query, or to perform calculations in the query.

Continues

7 Move the TotalPrice Field

Click the gray bar above the **TotalPrice** field to select the entire column. Drag the bar one column to the left to move it next to the **Quantity** column. (Move the field for ease of viewing after the calculation is done.)

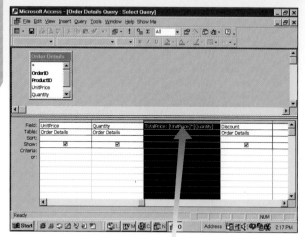

Drag

8 Preview Record Changes

When you have entered all the information for the calculation, you can preview the results. Click the **View** button on the toolbar.

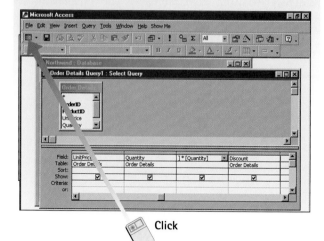

Click

9 Return to Design View

When you are done previewing the results of the expression, click the **View** button in the toolbar again to return to Design view. Make any required modifications to the query at this time.

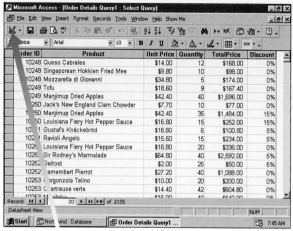

Click

10 Run the Query

In Design view, click the **Run** button on the toolbar to run the query. When you run the query, the changes you saw in the preview will actually be made by the query. The query will also be saved at this point, under the name you specified in an earlier step.

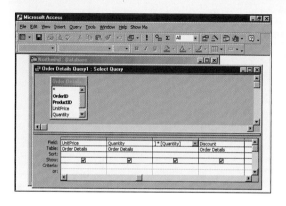

11 Save the Query

Close the query window and click **Yes** when you're prompted to save the query. When you open the **Order Details** table from the **Database** window, you will see the changes.

Click

End

How-To Hints

More on Query Criteria Expressions (Again?)

We told you about this earlier, but it bears repeating. You will find it tremendously helpful if you spend a little time reviewing information on criteria expressions.

To learn more about criteria expressions, go to the Contents tab in Access Help. Find the Using Criteria and Expressions to Retrieve Data folder within the Working with Queries folder.

More on Parameter Query Criteria

The brackets surrounding the criteria expression, in the Criteria field of the Design grid, are what make the Enter Parameter Value dialog box pop up when the query is run. You can specify many expressions (in the Criteria field of the Design grid) for the query to search for. For more information on criteria expressions, go to the Contents tab in Access Help. Find the Using Criteria and Expressions to Retrieve Data folder within the Working with Queries folder.

How to Create a Parameter Query

A *parameter query* is useful when the criteria frequently changes. A parameter query displays a dialog box when you open the query. The user enters the parameters and the matching records appear in Datasheet view. In this task, you'll design a query to list the **Northwind** database's suppliers by country—and the country you want to view varies.

Begin

1 Show the Query Objects

With the **Northwind** sample database open to the **Database** window, click the **Queries** button on the **Objects** bar to show the list of objects in queries.

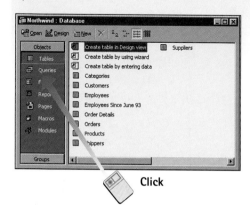

Click

2 Open a New Simple Query

On the **Database** window toolbar, click **New** to open the **New Query** dialog box.

Click

3 Start the Simple Query Wizard

Select **Simple Query Wizard** from the list on the right side of the **New Query** dialog box and click **OK**.

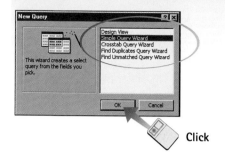

Click

4 Select the Query Fields

From the **Tables/Queries** list in the wizard dialog box, select the table from which you want to choose fields for your new query (**Table: Suppliers**). From the **Available Fields** pane, select the fields from which you want to retrieve data (click the >> button to select all the fields). Click **Next**.

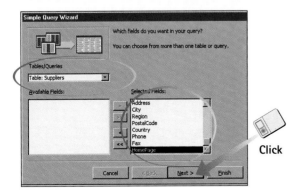

Click

5 Name the Query

In the text box on the next wizard pane, type a name for the new query. Select the **Modify the query design** option and click **Finish**. The query appears in Design view.

6 Enter the Criteria

In the bottom pane, scroll to the right until the **Country** field is in view. In the **Criteria** cell for the **Country** field, type [Which Country?].

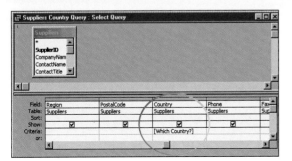

7 Run the Query

To preview the query, click the **View** button on the toolbar. Type Germany in the **Enter Parameter Value** dialog box and click **OK**. The query results are shown in Datasheet view. After saving the query, you can use it again by opening it from the **Queries Objects list**.

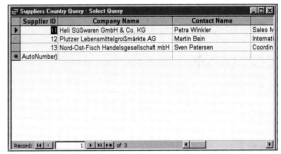

How-To Hints

Entering Parameter Values

When entering parameter values, be sure you understand that values are not case-sensitive (e.g., "germany" equals "Germany"). But also remember that misspellings or typos will not return results (e.g., "usa" does not equal "united states" or "america").

End

Project 3

Creating a Relational Database

Access 2000 is a *relational database application*. This means that it allows you to relate data in one table to data in one or more other tables. This capability saves you time and hard drive space by doing away with the need for redundant data. You can keep your tables focused so that they contain only the information you want them to contain. The relationships you define in your tables can be used to seek out the data you need with the use of *queries* (see Part 5, "Working with Database Table Queries"). Relationships also allow you to isolate related data in one or more tables by using multitable queries, which can summarize the data drawn from the selected tables. For more information on this advanced topic, see *Sams Teach Yourself Microsoft Access 2000 in 21 Days* (published by Sams Publishing).

In this project, you'll create a database that contains two tables: a Christmas card list and an email groups list. The first table contains the basic address information (name, address, and so on); the second table contains the email addresses and email groups. Then you'll learn how to use the relationships to access the data more efficiently.

After you have built your relational database, you'll be able to use the other tasks in this book to leverage other Access features to your advantage.

1 Create a Blank Database

Open Access. In the **Startup** dialog box, select **Blank Access database** and click **OK**.

2 Name the Database

In the **File New Database** dialog box, type a name for the database you are going to create in the **File name** text box. For this example, type **HolidayandEmailContacts**. Click **Create**. The **Database** window for your newly created database opens.

3 Open the Table Wizard

From the Objects bar, click **Tables**. From the Objects list in the right pane, double-click **Create table by using wizard** to begin creating the first table of your new database.

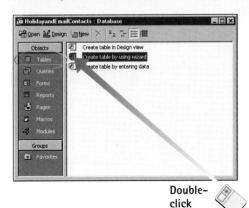

Double-
click

4 Choose a Sample Table

When the Table Wizard opens, select the **Personal** radio button as the table category. Because you are creating an address list, choose **Addresses** from the **Sample Tables** list.

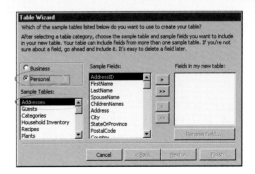

5 Select the Table Fields

Select the following fields from the **Sample Fields** list: FirstName, LastName, Address, City, StateOrProvince, PostalCode, and Country. When these fields appear in the **Fields in my new table** list, click **Next**.

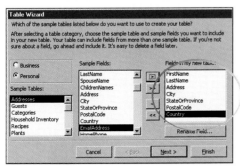

Continues

How-To Hints

Table Trivia

You determine the number and the names for the tables in your database based on the information you want to store and how you want to retrieve it. A good rule of thumb is to store the data in its smallest logical part (for example, follow our lead and use **FirstName** and **LastName** fields, rather than just a **Name** field).

6 Name the New Table

In the next wizard pane, type a name for the table whose specifications you just provided. For this example, type **ChristmasCardList**. Click **Next**.

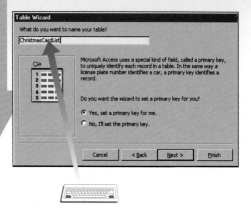

7 Enter Table Data

The wizard then asks how you want the table to be opened. Select **Enter data directly into the table** and click **Finish**. When the table opens, type three or four records as shown. Close the table. If Access prompts you to save the changes to the table, choose **Yes**.

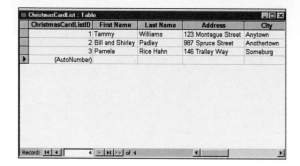

8 Start Another Table

To begin creating the second table of your new database, double-click **Create table by using wizard** in the **Tables** objects list in the **Database** window.

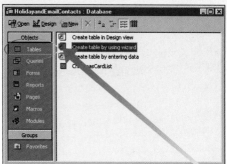

Double-click

9 Choose a Sample Table

When the Table Wizard opens, select the **Personal** radio button as the table category. Because this second table is going to be an email address list, select **Addresses** from the **Sample Tables** list.

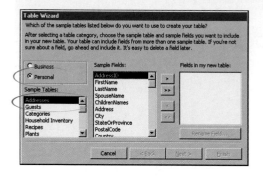

10 Select the Table Fields

Select the following fields from the **Sample Fields** list: **AddressID**, **FirstName**, **LastName**, **EmailAddress**, and **Nickname**. Highlight the **Nickname** field in the **Fields in my new table** list and click **Rename Field**. Change the field name to **EmailGroup** and click **OK**. Click **Next**.

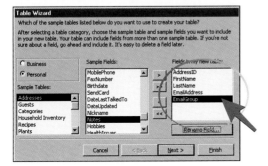

11 Name the New Table

In the next wizard pane, type a name for the table whose properties you have just defined. For this example, type **EmailGroups**. Click **Next**. The wizard then asks you about the relationship between this table and the other table in your database. Because you plan to define the relationship later, skip this step for now by clicking **Next**.

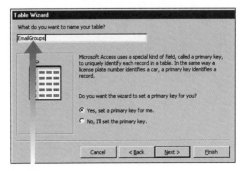

12 Enter Table Data

The wizard then asks how you want the table to be opened. Select **Enter data directly into the table** and click **Finish**. When the table opens, type three or four records as shown. Close the table. If Access prompts you to save the changes to the table, choose **Yes**.

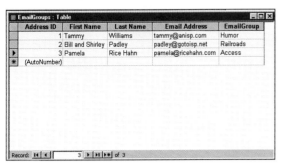

Continues

How-To Hints

Subdatasheets

As you explore the fields you've designed for your tables, you'll discover that Access can automatically create a subdatasheet (such as when two tables are related through a lookup field) or you can create your own subdatasheet. (See Part 4, Task 5, "How to Establish Table Relationships.") When you view a table in Datasheet view for which subdatasheets exist, you see plus marks (+) to the left of each name (record) in that table. When you click the +, you see the subdatasheet. Click the resulting − to hide that information again.

13 Begin Defining Relationships

To begin defining table relationships, make sure that all tables in the database are closed. The only window that should be open is the **Database** window. Remember that you establish a *relationship* between two tables when you connect a field with unique values in one table with a similar field in another table.

14 Open the Relationships Window

Click the **Relationships** button on the toolbar to open the **Relationships** window. The **Show Table** dialog box also appears.

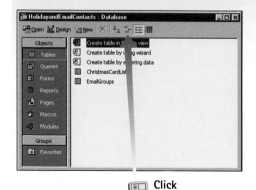

🖱 Click

15 Choose the Tables to Relate

In the **Show Table** dialog box, double-click **ChristmasCardList** and **EmailGroups** to add each table to the **Relationships** window. Click **Close** to close the **Show Table** dialog box.

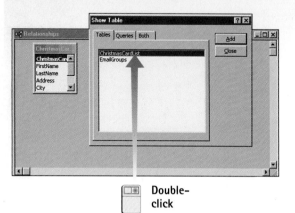

🖱 Double-click

Continues

How-To Hints

Primary Key

A *primary key* is a field or combination of fields that provides unique identification for each record in a table. For more information on this topic, read *Sams Teach Yourself Microsoft Access 2000 in 21 Days* (published by Sams Publishing).

16 Examine the Relationships Window

Notice that both tables appear in the **Relationships** window. A list of all the fields for each table appears in the table pane. Defining relationships between the tables is relatively easy from this point.

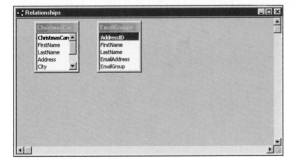

17 Relate the Fields

Determine the fields on which you want the tables to relate. Click and drag the field name from one table to the field name in the other table. In this example, you are relating the **ChristmasCardListID** field in the **ChristmasCardList** table to the **AddressID** field in the **EmailGroup** table. When you drop one field on the other, the **Edit Relationships** dialog box opens.

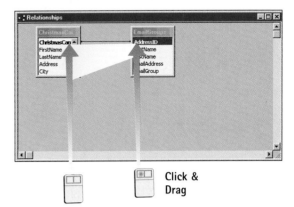

Click & Drag

18 Create the Relationship

In the **Edit Relationships** dialog box, click **Create New**. The relationship between these two tables is now defined, as you can see by the solid line that now connects the two tables.

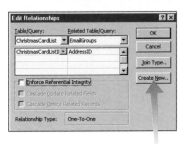

 Click

End

How-To Hints

Use Your Phone Keys as a Primary Key

As long as your address book doesn't contain separate records for a number of people that share some information in the same table (such as two separate entries for people who have the same phone number), consider using the phone number field as your primary key. Even if the residential phone number is the same for two people, you may still be able to keep things unique if you use their *cell* phone numbers.

Task

6

Creating and Working with Access Forms

*C*reating and using forms is one the basic functions you will use in Access 2000. It is important to learn the basics of forms because of the amount of time you'll spend using them. Think of a form as an attractive table. It holds all the same information as a table, but it's placed in a graphical-type window—one record at a time. The data you enter into a form is automatically placed into the table from which it gets its records.

In this part, you learn how to create forms with wizards and how to enter data into those forms. In addition, you'll discover how to format form fields, how to find and sort records, and how to customize and change form fields. ●

How to Create a Form Using AutoForm

AutoForm takes the hard work out of creating a new form. Using it ensures that all the necessary components are added to the new form. For the example used in this task, you've decided that your contacts list has gotten too large, and you want to create a separate form (called **Family**) to keep track of your family contacts.

Begin

1 Open the Database

Open the database in which you want to create a new form: Choose **File, Open** and click the filename of the database you want to open. Click **Open**.

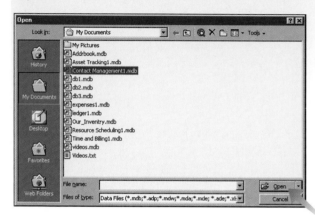

Click

2 Open the Forms Objects List

Access opens the database and displays the Switchboard. Press **F11** to bring the **Database** window forward, and click the **Forms** button in the Objects bar to open the **Forms Objects** list.

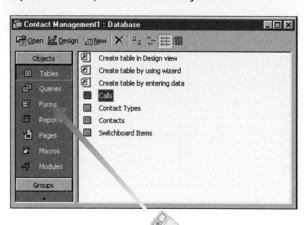

Click

3 Choose a New Form

Click the **New** button on the **Database** window toolbar to open the **New Form** dialog box.

Click

4 Select an AutoForm Wizard

Select one of the following AutoForm wizards: **Columnar, Tabular,** or **Datasheet.** When you click each wizard's name, look on the left side of the dialog box to see a small preview of that form type.

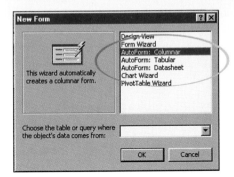

5 Select a Table or Query

Below the wizard list, select a table or query from which the new form's data will come. In this case, it's the **Contacts** table. Click **OK.**

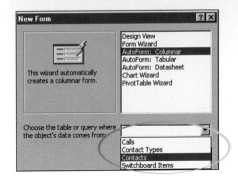

6 Name and Save the Form

Your new form appears on the screen. Click the **Save** button from the **Database** toolbar, type a form name in the **Save As** dialog box, and click **OK.**

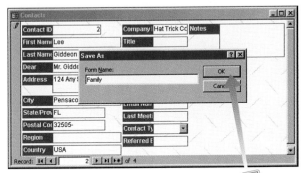

Click

End

How-To Hints

AutoForm Duplicates Data

Creating a new form in AutoForm duplicates all information within the table or query. It's easier to duplicate all the data automatically and then delete the fields or controls you don't need from the form.

AutoForm's Default Settings

Keep in mind that AutoForm uses, as a default, the settings used the last time the Form Wizard or AutoFormat was used. The screens shown in this task may appear different than those you see on your own screen.

How to Create a Form Using the Form Wizard

As with AutoForm, the Form Wizard simplifies the creation of a form. But the Form Wizard gives you more control over items such as fields, layout, and styles than AutoForm does. Also different from AutoForm is that you can choose fields from more than one table or query.

Begin

1 Click the Forms Button

Open the database in which you want to create a new form, and then click the **Forms** button on the Objects bar.

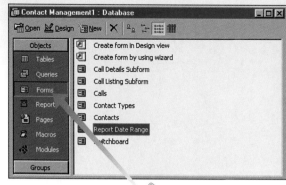

Click

2 Open the New Form Dialog

Click the **New** button on the **Database** window toolbar to open the **New Form** dialog box.

Click

3 Select the Form Wizard

Select **Form Wizard** from the list of available wizards in the **New Form** dialog box, and then click **OK**.

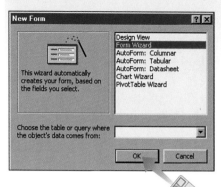

Click

4 Choose New Form Fields

Select a table or query from the **Tables/Queries** drop-down list. From the **Available Fields** pane, choose a field you want to appear in the new form and click the arrow button to place it in the **Selected Fields** pane. Repeat to add fields from more than one table or query. When you are done adding fields, click **Next**.

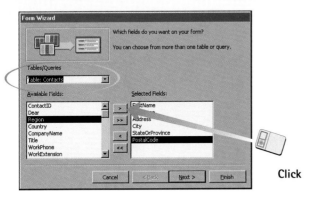

Click

5 Select a Layout

Choose one of the four layout options. Preview the layout on the left side of the wizard pane. Click **Next**.

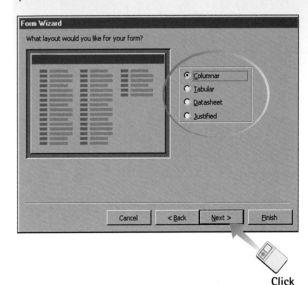

Click

6 Choose a Style

Select a style from the list. You can see what a style will look like on the left side of the wizard pane. Click **Next**.

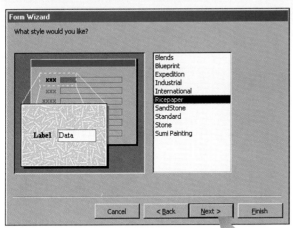

Click

7 Name and Open the Form

Type a title for your new form in the text box provided. Click the radio button next to **Open the form to view or enter information**. Click **Finish**.

Click

End

How to Enter Form Data

Databases would be useless without data, right? Entering data into a form is quite easy if you remember the Tab key on your keyboard. Otherwise you'll be clicking everything under the sun, trying to get the cursor in the correct place. In this task, you're entering data into your **Contact Management** database.

Begin

1 Open a Form

From the **Database** window, select a form from the **Forms Objects** list, and then click **Open** from the toolbar.

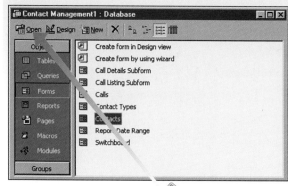

 Click

2 Start a New Record

If there is data in your table (and hence in the form), click the **New Record** button (the one with an arrow and an asterisk) at the bottom of the form to open a new record.

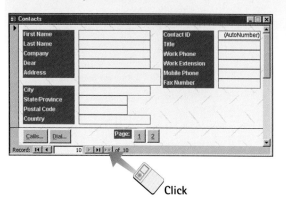

Click

3 Enter the First Field Data

The form opens with the cursor in the first field. Enter the appropriate data for this field.

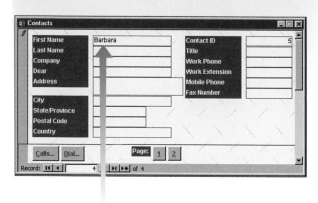

4 Press the Tab Key

With the data for the first field entered, press the **Tab** key on your keyboard. The cursor moves to the correct place in the next field.

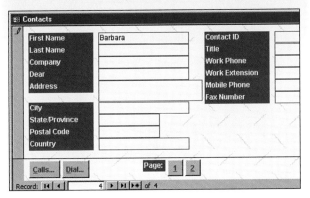

5 Fill Out the Other Fields

Enter data into as many other fields as you want, remembering to press the **Tab** key after each field. Add new records if you want, using the procedure outlined in Steps 2 through 5.

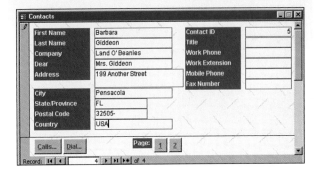

6 Save the Form

When you have finished your data entry, click the **Save** button on the Database toolbar.

Click

End

How-To Hints

Leaving Empty Fields

In the form in this task, you can leave some fields empty if you want. You can add data to those fields later. Remember that when you created the table the form is based on, you could set properties for the fields in the table. One of those properties was the **Required** property; if that property was set to **No**, you are not required to enter data into that field in the form.

How to Format Form Fields

Why keep the same old fonts and styles that everyone else uses? In Access, you can format individual form fields any way you want. Fonts, styles, colors, and alignment—the choices are almost endless. To format all fields the same way, you must select and format each field individually.

Begin

1 Choose a Font

With a form open and a field selected, select a new font from the **Font** drop-down list box on the **Formatting** toolbar.

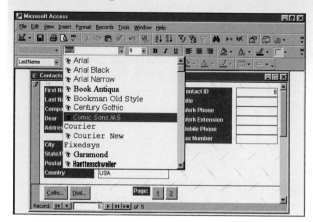

2 Resize the Text

To enlarge or shrink the text in a form field, select a size from the **Font Size** box on the **Formatting** toolbar.

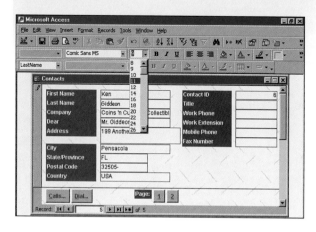

3 Apply Special Text Styles

To make the text in a field bold, italicized, or underlined, click the appropriate button on the **Formatting** toolbar. In this case, choose **Bold**.

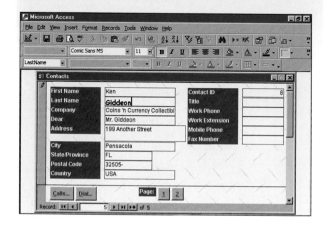

4 Realign the Text

You have the choice of making the text in fields left-aligned, right-aligned, or centered. Click the appropriate button on the **Formatting** toolbar. In this case, choose **Center**.

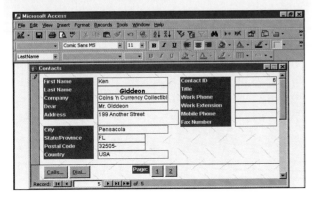

5 Set a Field's Background Color

You can change a field's background color by choosing a color from the pop-up menu under the **Fill/Back Color** button on the **Formatting** toolbar. Click the arrow next to the button to display the pop-up menu.

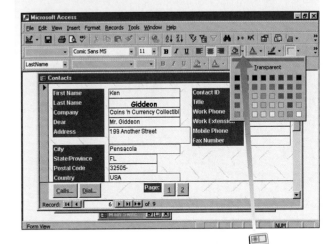

Click

6 Set the Text Color

To change the text color for a field, click the arrow next to the **Font/Fore Color** button and choose a color from the pop-up menu.

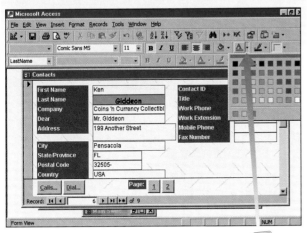

Click

End

How-To Hints

Allow Design Changes Property in Forms

At times, you may attempt format changes that don't work in Form view. If this occurs, click the **Form Selector** (the right arrow in the upper-left corner of the Form window) and click the **Properties** button on the Database toolbar. Scroll to the bottom of the **All** tab and change **Allow Design Changes** to **All Views**.

Changes Affect All Records Within a Form

Keep in mind that any formatting changes you make in a form's field will also change the same field on other records within the form you have opened. The table data itself is not affected by the formatting you apply to the form.

TASK 5

How to Find and Sort Records in a Form

The number of records in a form can become quite large very quickly. Learning how to find and sort records in a form is essential if you are to keep your sanity when dealing with forms.

Begin

1 Select a Search Field

In the form, place the cursor in the field you want to search within. In this example you want to search by last name, so select the **Last Name** field. Click the **Find** button (the binoculars) on the **Database** toolbar.

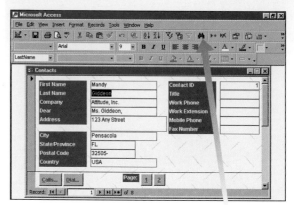

Click

2 Type a Search Value

Type a search value in the **Find What** field in the **Find and Replace** dialog box. In this example, you're looking for the last name *Hahn*.

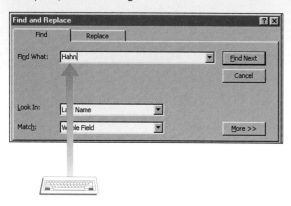

3 Set Find Options

If you want, you can change the field you're searching from the **Look In** pull-down menu. From the **Match** pull-down menu, make a selection (**Any Part of Field** is usually the best choice).

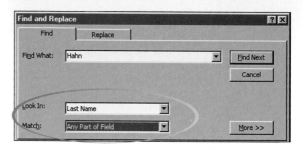

162 PART 6: CREATING AND WORKING WITH ACCESS FORMS

4 Start the Search

Click **Find Next** to begin the records search. Matching records appear in the form, or you'll receive a message stating that Access was unable to find an item fitting your description.

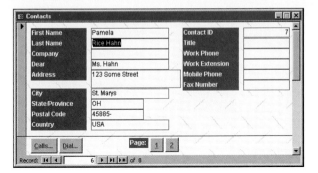

5 Select a Sort Field

If you want to sort your form's records, decide by which field you want them sorted. Click that field in the form to select it. In this example, you're going to sort by last name.

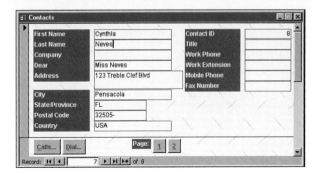

6 Sort the Records

Now you're ready to sort records. Decide whether you want the sort to be ascending (A to Z) or descending (Z to A). Click the appropriate button on the **Database** toolbar. The records are now sorted in the order you want.

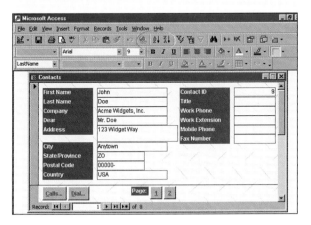

How-To Hints

Records Navigation

You can browse form records with the navigation buttons at the bottom of the form. These buttons allow you to move forward or backward one record at a time, or to the first or last record in the form. If you know the record number, you can type it in the record number box and go there directly by pressing **Enter**.

End

Project 4

Creating a Custom Form

In this project, we're going to use Design view to create a database. Although Access 2000 makes it easy to store your data, it can't always predict how best to store that information. For that, you need to do some planning before you start creating your fields and keying in information. That's not to say you have to get it perfect the first time out. After you create a database and work with it, you'll see where improvements can be made or think of additional fields that should be included. Access 2000 provides ways to make changes after you've created the database. However, you'll lessen the odds of massive changes (and the resulting additional work) if you get out a pen and brainstorm on paper before you start.

What? Odds are, what you create isn't going to be perfect! Yep. Deal with it. In life, you dive in, get your feet wet, and eventually master the strokes that get you from one side of the pond to the other. As with anything else in life, your database skills will evolve once you get in there and do it. Does a baby stick to crawling just because he falls the first time he attempts to walk? Of course not. However, that baby usually has somebody there to hold his hand when he needs it. If he's lucky, he has somebody on each side of him. (This book has two authors. Coincidence?)

We covered many of the ground rules in the first three projects. Sure, you'll continue to learn more skills, but let's loosen up and have some fun together while you do so.

1 Put Pen to Paper

For this project one of the authors, Pam, decides that she needs a better record of her video-tape titles than the list she maintains as a Word file. Part of the early database planning she does involves listing field name possibilities. Tape title is the obvious first choice.

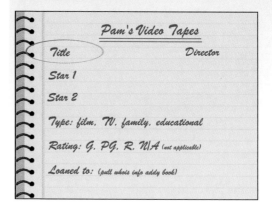

2 Fine-Tune the Fields

Other potential fields to include are the stars, director, rating, type (because Pam has film, TV, and family tapes in her collection), and a "loaned to" category (because Pam is generous *and* forgetful). She also decides to list the male star and the female star. Later, if she wants to see how many Tom Hanks or Meg Ryan films are in her collection, she can limit such searches to a single field.

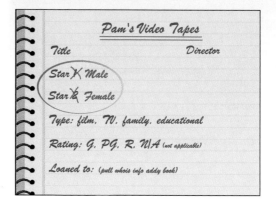

3 The Plot Thickens

Pam decides to include a record of whether the tape was purchased or taped from TV. Plus, because Pam keeps films on hand for the MBABGDITW (Most Beautiful and Brilliant Granddaughter in the World) and the MHABGSITW (Most Handsome and Brilliant Grandson in the World), she decides to add *Disney* to the Type category.

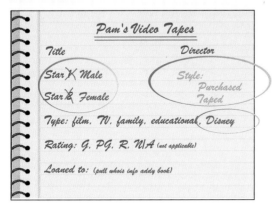

4 A Hit with the Reality Stick

After giving it some thought, Pam realizes she probably won't update the database each time she loans out a tape. More than likely, she'll just stick a Post-It note on her printed report. So she crosses off the "loaned to" field. However, she decides to include the year the film was made or recorded.

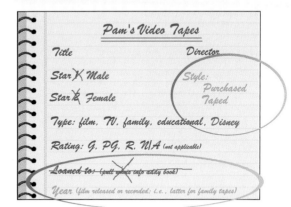

5 Ready to Roll

By now, Pam's notebook looks as messy as the top of her desk. However, after she adds *AutoNumber* and *Notes* fields and assigns order numbers to those fields, she decides she's ready to begin actually creating the database. In the following steps, we show you how to implement Pam's ideas into your own database design.

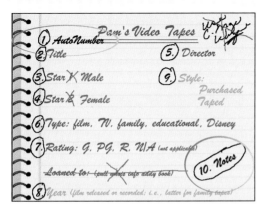

Continues

How-To Hints

Points to Ponder

Here are some questions you should ask yourself when you're planning your database:

✓ What is the source of your data? Can you import it (see Project 5, "Importing Data into an Access Table," or Task 11 in Part 3, "Creating and Working with Database Files"), or do you have to type it all in?

✓ Which of the tasks will be repetitive? (There are ways to simplify data entry that we'll discuss in Project 5.)

✓ What type of printed reports will you want to generate from the information?

✓ Will other people be using the database?

✓ Do you need to password-protect this information? If so, will you want to prevent others from viewing it? Or do you just want to prevent them from making changes?

6 Houston, We Have Liftoff

To open Access from the **Start** menu, choose **Programs, Microsoft Access**.

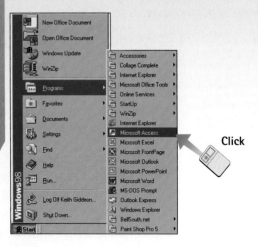

Click

7 Ready to Rumble

From the Microsoft Access **Startup** dialog box, select **Blank Access database** and click **OK**.

8 Pick a Filename

In the **File New Database** dialog box, type the filename you want to assign to your database (for this example, type **videos**). Microsoft Access 2000 automatically adds the .MDB file extension. Click **Create**.

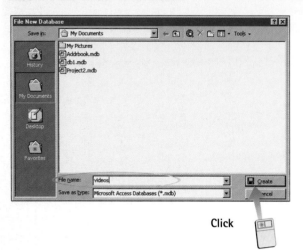

Click

9 Create Your Table

The database opens with **Tables** selected in the Objects bar. The right pane of the **videos: Database** window shows three new object shortcuts. Double-click the icon next to **Create table in Design view**.

Double-click

10 Name the Fields

On the first line of the **Table1: Table** window, type the first field name (in this case, **Tape Number**). Press the **Tab** key.

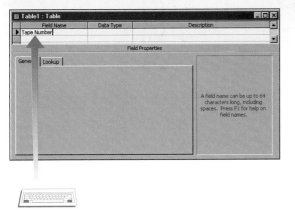

11 Use Data Types

In the **Data Type** column, click the **down arrow** button to see the choices (discussed in Project 1, "Northwind Sample Database Tutorial," and Task 2 in Part 4, "Creating and Working with Access Tables"). Select **AutoNumber**.

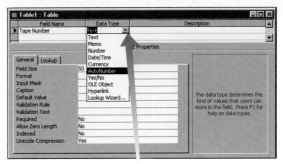

 Click

12 The Description Option

Entering information in the **Description** column is optional, so we'll skip that for now. Press the **Tab** key to go to the **Field Name** column. Type the next six field names on your list (see the Hints box for help). Each of these fields will be the **Text** data type by default, so you can just type the field name and press **Tab** three times.

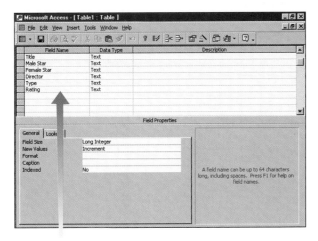

How-To Hints

Help with Data Types

If you are uncertain about which data type to select, you can press F1 to display the Help file for that property before you make your selection.

Help with Step 12

If you're following this example word-for-word, here's a list of the "next six field names" you're asked to enter in Step 12:

Field Name	Data Type
Title	Text
Male Star	Text
Female Star	Text
Director	Text
Type	Text
Rating	Text

Continues

13 The Date/Time Data Type

Now type **Year** for the field name. From the **Data Type** drop-down list, select **Date/Time**. Use this data type rather than **Text** so that you'll be consistent when you enter the date that a family tape was recorded; consistency is important for search queries. Press **Tab** twice.

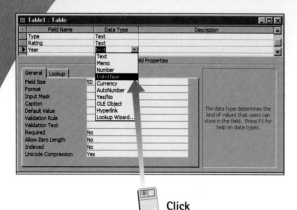

Click

14 Keep Refining

It's okay to change your mind as you create a database, especially if you believe the changes will improve your database design. Rather than use the name Style for field 9, you decide to use the field name **Purchased** and then use **Yes/No** for the **Data Type**. You can also type text in the **Description** column as a reminder for what you should enter in that field. In this case, type **Yes designates a commercial film video; No is one I taped myself** and press **Tab** once.

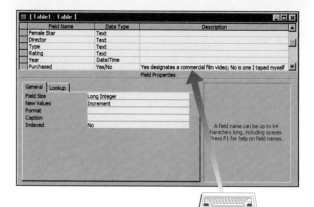

15 Name Your Table

Type **Notes** as the final field name. On the toolbar, click the **Save** icon. The **Save As** dialog box prompts you to assign a name to your table. Type the name in the **Table Name** box (in this case, type **Pam's Video Tapes**). Click **OK**.

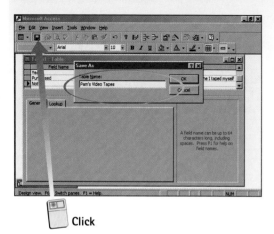

Click

16 The Primary Key

Access prompts you to select a primary key to help define the relationship between this table and others in a database. A primary key isn't required and is unnecessary as long as this table is the only one in the database. However, to be ready in case your database evolves to include other tables, it's a good idea to include a primary key. Click **Yes**.

Click

17 Change the Primary Key

Access automatically sets the first field in your database (Tape Number) as the primary key. But you want the primary key to be the Title field. To make that change, right-click the Tape Number box and deselect the Primary Key option.

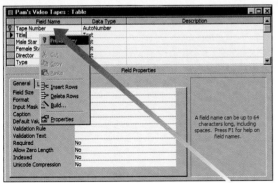

Right-click

18 Set the New Primary Key

Right-click the Title box and select the Primary Key option to make this field the primary key.

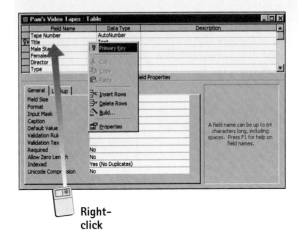

Right-click

19 Exit Table Design

Click the Close box (the X in the upper-right corner of the Table window) to exit the table design. You are prompted to save any changes if you haven't done so already.

20 Open the Newly Created Table

Your new table now appears in the Objects list of the Database window. Double-click the icon to the left of the Pam's Video Tapes table name. The table opens.

Double-click

Continues

21 Enter Film Information

Enter some video information into the database table. Press **Tab** to pass the first field (and let Access automatically number that field) and type **Picture Perfect** in the **Title** field. Enter **Jay Mohr**, **Jennifer Aniston**, **Glen Gordon Caron**, **Film**, and **PG-13** in the next five fields, pressing **Tab** between entries.

22 Enter Film's Production Year

When you get to the **Year** field, note that you must enter a month and a year separated by a slash. The **Date/Time** data type you assigned to this field in Step 13 requires you to provide information in a certain format. The field will not allow you to enter just a year; if you don't know or need the exact date, you must still type a month and a year (such as **1/97**) and press **Tab**. Notice that Access automatically updates what you type to display 1/1/97.

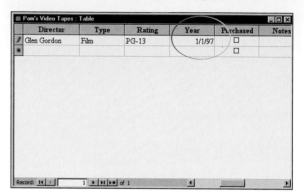

23 Select Purchased Check Box

Note that the **Purchased** field contains a check box. Recall that you assigned the **Yes/No** data type to this field in Step 14. Because the video *Picture Perfect* was indeed purchased and not recorded at home, click the box to place a check mark in it. Press **Tab** and enter any notes in the next field. Repeat Steps 21, 22, and 23 to enter more information about your video collection.

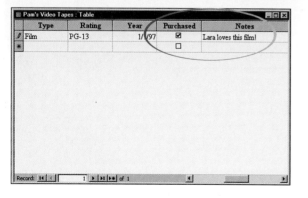

How-To Hints

You Can Find Almost Any Info Online

Can't read the fine print on the tape package and need to confirm how a film star spells his or her name or what year a film was made? Check out The Internet Movie Database at http://us.imdb.com/.

24 Adjust a Field's Width

You can easily adjust the width of a field. Move the mouse over the gray field name bar until the pointer changes to a vertical line with left and right arrows. Double-click on the right side of the bar. The width of the field automatically adjusts to accommodate the text in that field.

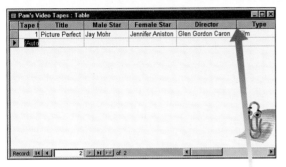

Double-
click

25 We're Off to See the Wizard

In the Objects bar in the **Database** window, click **Forms**. Although you could create a form from scratch, Access makes it easy with the wizard. You've already determined your fields. Double-click **Create form by using wizard** to open the **Form Wizard** dialog box.

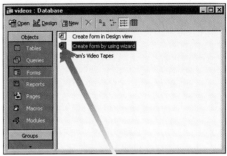

Double-
click

26 Select Fields for the Form

In the **Form Wizard** dialog box, click the >> button to move all the entries from the **Available Fields** pane in the **Selected Fields** pane. Click **Next**.

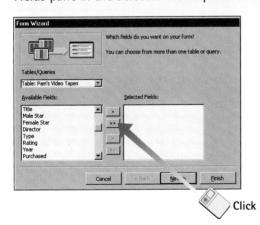

Click

27 Select the Form's Layout

The Form Wizard asks what layout you would like for your form. The choices are **Columnar**, **Tabular**, **Datasheet**, and **Justified**. In this case, the choice is **Columnar**, but you can experiment by clicking the options. When you have made a selection, click **Next**.

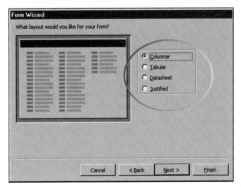

Continues

28 Select a Style

The Form Wizard asks what style you would like. Click the options to view the different styles available. When you have made a choice, click Next. (In this case the choice is Blends.)

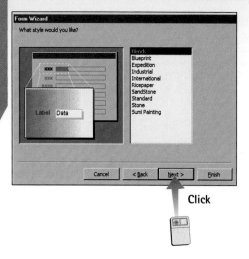

Click

29 Finish the Wizard

Type a new name for the form or accept the default name proposed by the wizard and then click Finish. The wizard automatically opens your form for you when it's done. Look at the form and click the Close box when you are done.

30 Open the Table in Design View

You've determined that you meant to select Memo as the data type for the Notes field instead of Text. (The Memo data type allows you to enter much more information than the Notes data type.) Click Tables in the Objects bar, select the table from the Objects list, and click the Design button in the Database window toolbar.

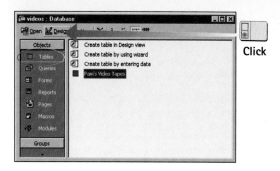

Click

31 Change a Data Type

In the Table window, move down to the Notes line. In the Data Type column for that line, click the down arrow next to Text and select Memo to make the change. Click the Save icon to save the database table.

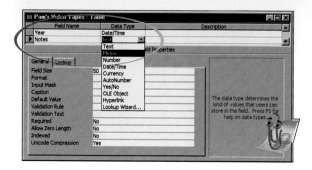

32 Change a Field Name

To return to the Datasheet view. Click the **Datasheet View** icon on the toolbar. If you want to change a field name, move the mouse over a column until the pointer changes to a down arrow and then double-click and type a new column name.

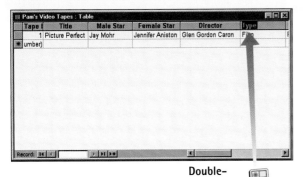

Double-click

33 Simple Sort Options

Move the mouse pointer over a column head so that it changes to a down arrow and then right-click. Notice that you can sort the column in descending or ascending alphabetical order. With a simple database, these sorting options may suffice. If so, congratulations! Continue entering data for *your* database of video tapes (in the Objects bar in the Database window, select **Forms** and double-click **Pam's Video Tapes** to open the entry form you created earlier in this project).

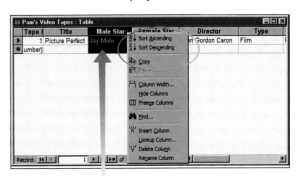

Right-click

End

How-To Hints

Database Buzzwords

You've encountered a number of database buzzwords in this project. Here's a list to help you remember them and their meanings:

Table   The part of the database that stores details about a class of information or facts. (The Contact Manager database example in Project 2, "Exploring Access Database Wizards," had three tables; the Videos database in this project has only one table.)

Field   An Access 2000 table stores each fact in a field. (The Videos database in this project has 10 fields.)

Form   The area in which you can enter, edit, and view information. (In Form view, you see one record at a time; in Datasheet view, you see all the records and often have to scroll sideways to look at them all.)

Report   A summary of a database or a table intended to be printed.

Task

Creating Access Reports

*R*eports are valuable when you need to share your database data with other people. The data in a report, which is most often generated from a table or query, is presented in a way that is more appealing than the spreadsheet-table format we associate with the term *database*. Access reports can hold their own in today's world of glamorous printed reports.

In this part of the book, you learn how to create reports using wizards, how to sort the records within Access reports, and how to modify the design of your report even after it has been created.

How to Create a Report Using AutoReport

AutoReport allows you to select one record source (a table or a query) and then creates your report using the last settings from the Report Wizard (see Task 2). The Columnar and Tabular AutoReports are similar to AutoReport except that they produce a specific layout (columnar and tabular, respectively). You can later change a report's appearance and options in Design view, as described in Task 4.

Begin

1 Open the Database

Open the database in which you want to create a new report. In this task, we're using **Time and Billing1**, created using the skills in Part 3, Task 3. To open the database, choose **File, Open**; select the filename of the database you want to open and click **Open**.

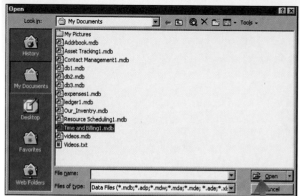

Click

2 Choose Reports

On the Objects bar in the **Database** window, click the **Reports** button to open the Reports Objects list.

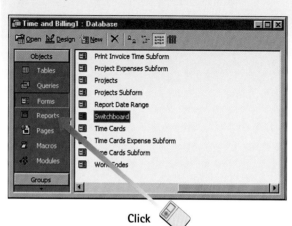

Click

3 Choose a New Report

Click the **New** button on the **Database** window toolbar to open the **New Report** dialog box.

Click

4 Select an AutoReport Wizard

Select one of the two AutoReport options: **Columnar** or **Tabular**. Click each one and look at the sample in the left pane of the dialog box.

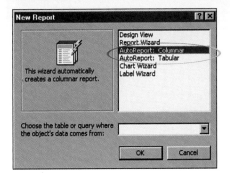

5 Select a Table or Query

From the drop-down list at the bottom of the dialog box, select the table or query from which the new report's data will come. Click **OK**.

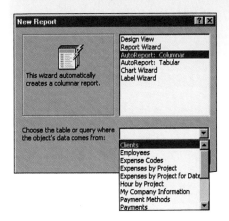

6 Name and Save the Report

The new report appears onscreen. Choose **File, Save** and enter a report name in the **Save As** dialog box. Click **OK**.

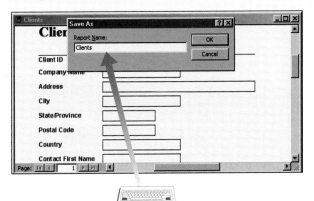

End

How-To Hints

AutoForm Duplicates Data

Creating a new report with AutoReport displays all information from the selected table or query. The report is opened in Print Preview. If you want to print the report, simply click the **Print** icon or choose **File, Print**. For more on Print Preview and printing, see Task 5 later in this part.

How to Create Reports Using Report Wizard

Just like AutoReport, the Report Wizard simplifies the creation of a report, but it also gives you more control over items such as fields, layout, and styles. Also different from AutoReport is that the Report Wizard lets you sort the order of records in the new report.

Begin

1 Open the Database

To open the database in which you want to create a new report, choose **File, Open** and select the filename of the database. Click **Open**. (If you already have a database open, just open that database's **Database** window.)

Click

2 Choose Reports

Click the **Reports** button on the Objects bar to open the Reports Objects list.

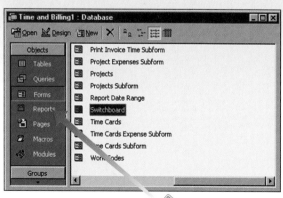

Click

3 Open the New Reports Dialog Box

Click **New** from the **Database** window toolbar to open the **New Reports** dialog box.

Click

4 Select the Wizard

Select **Report Wizard** from the list of options in the **New Report** dialog box and click **OK**.

Click

5 Select a Table or Query

From the **Tables/Queries** drop-down list box in the **Report Wizard** dialog box, select the table or query from which the new report's data will come.

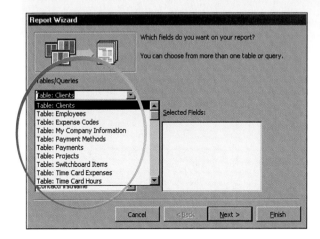

6 Choose Fields

From the **Available Fields** pane, select a field you want in the new report and click the > button to place it in the **Selected Fields** pane. Repeat Steps 5 and 6 to add fields from more than one table or query. Click **Next**.

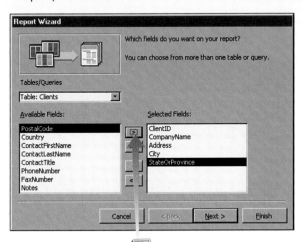

Click

7 Add Grouping Levels

Grouping levels can be compared to indented headers. The fields you select as grouping levels stand out from the rest of the records. You can select up to four grouping levels. Click the **up arrow** and **down arrow** buttons to change the priority of the levels. Click **Next**.

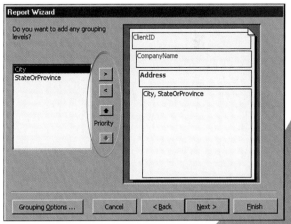

Continues

8 Select Sort Orders

In the first drop-down box, select the field you want to use to sort the records. Change the sort order by clicking the sort button next to the drop-down box. Select **(None)** to leave the report in the already established database sort order and to include more information in the report. Click **Next**.

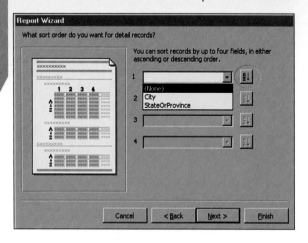

9 Choose a Layout

From the **Layout** box, select a layout format. Access displays a preview of your choice on the left side of the dialog box.

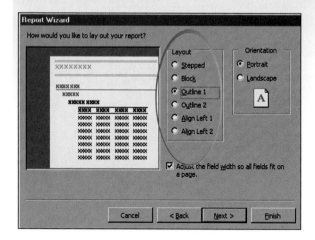

10 Select Report Orientation

From the **Orientation** box, select a report orientation (**Portrait** or **Landscape**). This is the same as choosing paper orientation in Page Setup of most Windows applications. Click **Next**.

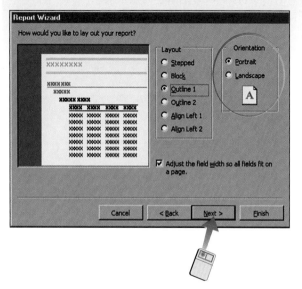

11 Pick a Style

Select a style for your report. Access provides a preview of your choice on the left side of the dialog box. Click **Next**.

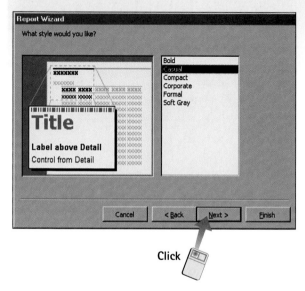

Click

12 Title and Open the Report

Type a title for your new report. Select the **Preview the report** option and click **Finish**. Your report opens in Print Preview.

End

How-To Hints

Selecting Fields

You can use the **>>** button to quickly select all the fields in the **Available Fields** pane. Use the **<** button to remove the few fields you don't want to include in your report. This shortcut is quicker and easier than selecting all the fields individually when you want to include most but not all of the available fields in your report.

How the Sort Buttons Work

The sort button with A on top of Z sorts in ascending order (from 0 to 9 and from A to Z). The sort button with Z on top of A sorts in descending order (from 9 to 0 and from Z to A).

Do a Test Printout

Make sure that your printer can adequately handle any special formatting you add to your reports. Sometimes special effects such as boxes with drop shadows look great on your screen but don't show up as good on paper. Therefore, it's a good idea to print a sample page before you print the entire report so you'll know if you should make any formatting changes.

How to Sort Records in a Report

Access makes it easy to sort the records in a report you have created. Whether you want your records sorted from A to Z or from Z to A, with Access, record sorting is a valuable tool to have. You select the fields to be sorted and the manner in which you want them sorted, and Access takes care of the rest.

Begin

1 Open in Design View

Open the database that contains the report you want to work with. In the Objects bar in the **Database** window, click the **Reports** button and select the report you want to work with from the Objects list. Click the **Design** button on the **Database** window toolbar.

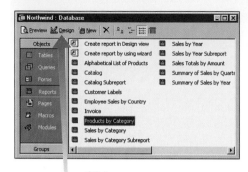

Click

2 Choose Sorting and Grouping

Click the **Sorting and Grouping** button on the toolbar to display the **Sorting and Grouping** dialog box.

Click

3 Select the First Sort Level

Click the first field to activate the drop-down arrow. Click the arrow. From the list that appears, select the field by which you want the records in your report to be sorted.

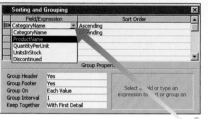

Click

4 Choose the First Sort Order

In the second column of the dialog box, select the sort order. Click the drop-down arrow; from the list that appears, select **Ascending** or **Descending,** depending on how you want the records to be sorted.

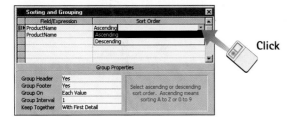

Click

5 Add Sort Levels

To further sort records, you can add more sort levels. Click in the second row of the dialog box and repeat Steps 3 and 4 to select the secondary sort field. Continue adding as many sort levels as necessary.

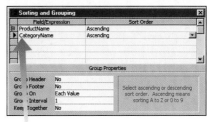

 Click

6 Change the Sort Order

Click the **Close box** on the **Sorting and Grouping** dialog box. Click the **Save** button on the toolbar and then click the **View** button on the toolbar. If prompted to save your work, choose **OK**. You can now view the sorted report.

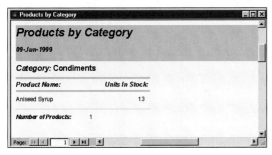

End

How-To Hints

Multi-Level Sorts

Access sorts records based on the order of the fields you set up in the **Sorting and Grouping** dialog box. This feature can come in handy if you have fields that contain the same value (such as *Smith* in the **LastName** field). If you sort on just the **LastName** field, all the Smith records are grouped together. If you make the **FirstName** field the secondary sort field, Access sorts the records by last name and then by first name, arranging all the Smiths by their first names.

How to Modify a Report in Design View

You've created a report, added your records, and sorted them just the way you like. There's only one problem: You don't like the look and feel of the report now. A simple solution is to modify the report with the AutoFormat feature.

Begin

1 Open in Design View

With the **Reports** button selected on the Objects bar, click the report you want to modify in the Objects list. Then click the **Design** button on the **Database** window toolbar. The report appears in Design view.

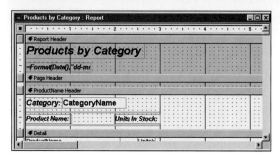

2 Open AutoFormat

Choose **Format, AutoFormat** to begin modifying your report.

3 Choose a New Format

Choose a new format from the list in the left pane of the **AutoFormat** dialog box. You can see a preview of your choice on the right side of the dialog box.

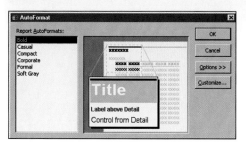

4 Select Attributes

Click the **Options** button. The **AutoFormat** dialog box lengthens to display several font attributes. Select or deselect the attributes and watch the effect your selections have on the sample text.

5 Select Customized Options

To make special formatting changes, click the **Customize** button. In the **Customize AutoFormat** dialog box, select one of the three options. To see what an option does, click it and read the tip window at the bottom of the dialog box. (If you want to change only the current report, do not change anything in this dialog box.) Click **OK** to close the dialog box and keep your changes.

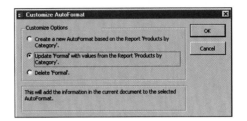

6 View the New Format

Click **OK** to close the **AutoFormat** dialog box and view the changes to your report. If it still doesn't meet your approval, repeat Steps 2 through 5.

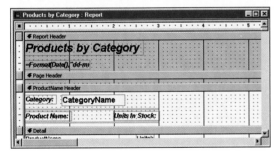

End

How-To Hints

Remember Your Audience

When you plan your report design, think *niche marketing*: a product presentation, such as a print ad or commercial, slanted to appeal to a specific demographic. The formatting choices that make up a good report design can be arbitrary. Not everyone has the same tastes. The specific purpose of your report determines whether it's best done in an informal style or whether it should be formatted for a more professional (stodgy) appearance.

How to Preview and Print a Report

After you're satisfied that your report contains the data you need, you should print it for the world to see. In this task, you preview a report from the **Northwind** sample database before you print it. Previewing lets you proof the report for errors and layout problems. After you preview, you print the report.

Begin

1 Open the Report Objects List

Open the **Northwind** sample database so that the **Database** window is visible. From the Objects bar, choose **Reports** to show the Objects list of reports available.

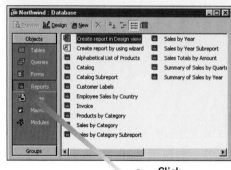

Click

2 Select the Report

From the Objects list, select the report you want to preview. For this example, select the **Sales by Category** report.

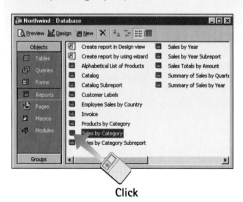

Click

3 Open the Preview

Click the **Preview** button on the Database window toolbar to preview the layout of the report. See the How-To Hints box at the end of this task for information about modifying the report if necessary.

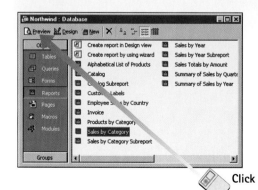

Click

4 Close the Preview

When you're through previewing the report but are not ready to print the report, click the **Close box** on the toolbar. The **Database** window reappears.

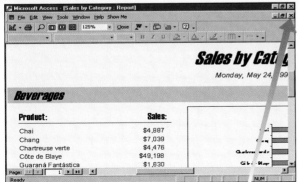

Click

5 Open the Print Dialog Box

Select **File, Print** to open the **Print** dialog box. Choose the desired settings for the printer, print range, and number of copies.

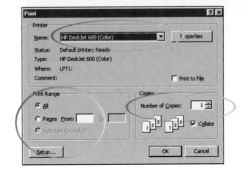

6 Print the Report

After choosing your printer settings, click **OK** to print the report.

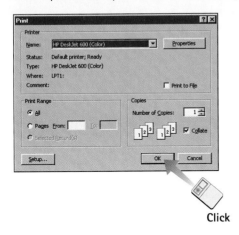

Click

End

How-To Hints

Modify the Report Before Printing

If you decide that you don't like the way your report looks, you can change it before you print it. Refer to Task 4, "How to Modify a Report in Design View," earlier in this part, for details.

Project 5

Working with an Access Table

This project works with the table you created in Project 4, "Creating a Custom Form." When you're done with this project, your videotape database will be a new and improved incarnation of the one from Project 4. As you're about to discover, you don't have to get hung up on the "proper" way to do something if another way is faster and gets the job done. You'll make a few modifications to your original table, and then, because of that efficiency factor, you get to delete it completely.

In the process, you'll learn how to import a file from an outside application (in this case, Microsoft Word) into a table. You'll also learn how to link tables. When you *import* data, Access creates a copy of it. Any changes you make to that data in Access don't show up in your original file. For example, if you delete a number in your electronic phone book, the change shows up only on *your* copy. Regardless of how many people have a copy of that same phone book, your change won't show up in any of those copies. On the other hand, when you *link* data, changes made to the original (source) file show up in the linked file, and vice versa. A link establishes a live connection between the files. Note that there is a difference between *table relationships* (or *relational databases*) and *linked tables*. And when you're done linking tables, you'll learn how to use a wizard to create reports that reference the data in the tables.

1 Open a Word File

Project 4 mentioned that Pam has a list of videotape titles she maintains in Word. To import that list into Access, you need to save it in an Access-friendly format. Open (or create) a similar list in Word.

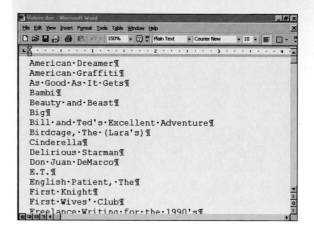

2 Save the Word File as Text

From the Word **File** menu, select **Save As**. From the drop-down menu in the **Save As** dialog box, select **Text Only (*.txt)**. Click **Save**. In this example, you save the Word file `Videos.doc` as `Videos.txt`. It isn't necessary to exit Word, but you must close the file you intend to import.

Click

3 Open the Project 3 Database

From the **Start** menu, choose **Programs**, **Microsoft Access**. You want to open the database file you created in Project 3, so from the **Startup** dialog box, click **Open an existing file**, choose **videos**, and click **OK**.

Click

4 Import the File

From the Microsoft Access **File** menu, select **Get External Data** and then select **Import**.

5 Set Import Window for Text Files

In the **Import** dialog box, go to the **Files of type** drop-down menu and choose **Text Files** (*.txt, *.csv, *.tab, *.asc).

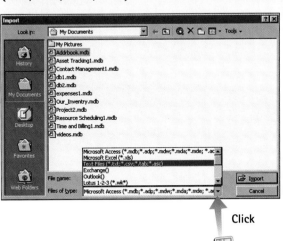

Click

6 Select Your Text File

Select the file you want to import by clicking it. Use the standard Windows browsing features in the dialog box to locate the file you want to open. In this case, select the file that you saved in Step 2 as Videos.txt. Click **Import**.

Click

Continues

7 The Import Text Wizard

The **Import Text Wizard** dialog opens automatically. Notice that the list of video titles from the Word file appears in the pane at the bottom of the window. Because you're not working with a delimited file, select **Fixed Width**. Click **Next**.

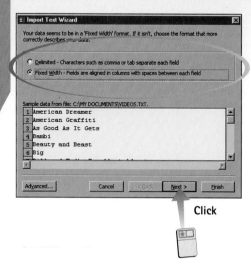

Click

8 Approve Line Breaks

The Import Text Wizard calculates where you'll want your line breaks. Follow the instructions given in this dialog box if you need to change the line breaks in your text file. Click **Next**.

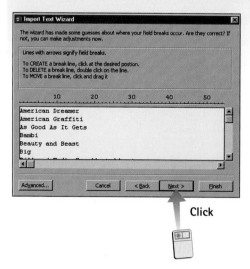

Click

9 Select the Location for the Imported Data

For your needs, it's quicker to import the text file into a new table than to make the changes necessary (by creating a comma- or tab-delimited file) to import it directly into the videos database. Select **In a New Table** and then click **Next**.

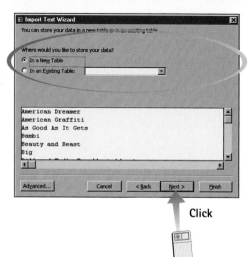

Click

How-To Hints

K.I.S.S. (Keep It Simple, Stupid)

For small amounts of data, it may be simpler to select and copy (Ctrl+C) that information in the original text file and then paste (Ctrl+V) it into your Access table than it is to import the data.

Do As We Say, Not...

In most cases, it's best to break your table fields into the smallest increments of data. That's why most address books have a **FirstName** and a **LastName** field. (You broke that rule in the videos.mdb example from Project 4 to keep things simple.)

10 Enter Field Options

The wizard prompts you to enter field options. (For those times when you need more information on Data Type and other field options—such as when the imported data will span several fields—see Part 4, Task 4, "How to Enter Data into a Table.") There is only a single column of data in the Word text file you are importing, so you have only one set of field options. Type **Title** in the **Field Name** box, select **No** in the **Indexed** box, and select **Text** in the **Data Type** box. Click **Next**.

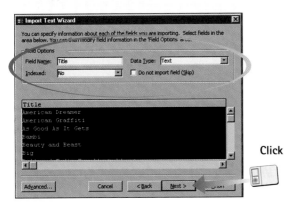

Click

11 Set the Primary Key

Access knows more about setting a primary key at this point than you do. (Notice that it has inserted a new ID field that numbers each line of the text file.) To let Access set our primary key, leave the default **Let Access add primary key** option selected and click **Next**.

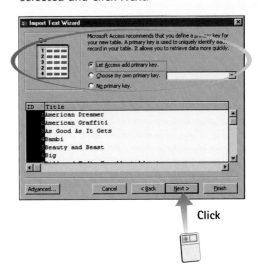

Click

12 Enter a Table Name

Because you're creating a new table for the data you're importing, type **Imported Video List**. If you want Access 2000 to do a performance analysis on the table you just created, select the **I would like a wizard to analyze my table after importing the data** option at the bottom of this dialog box. Click **Finish**.

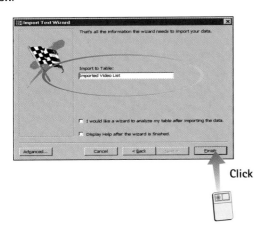

Click

Continues

How-To Hints

Field Options

Some field properties can change the way data is displayed and depend on the **Data Type** field (for example, the amount of text you can enter in a Text versus a Memo data type field). Other properties depend on how you want to manually adjust the appearance (such as a column width altered to accommodate the text entered in that field). See Part 4, Task 3, "How to Customize Access Tables," for more information.

13 A Good Sign

If all goes well, an alert box informs you that the wizard is finished importing the Word text file (***\videos.txt**) to the Access table (**Imported Video List**). (If all doesn't go well, don't panic! The Access 2000 wizard presents warning boxes that ask how you want to uncover any errors that hinder the import.) Click **OK**.

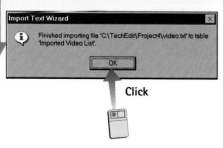

Click

14 Admire Your Work

In the **Database** window, double-click the icon next to **Imported Video List** to open the new table. Move the mouse pointer over the **Title** field until it changes to the vertical line with the left and right arrows. Double-click to expand the field to accommodate the width of the text. Save the file.

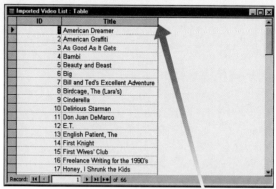

Double-click

15 Change to Design View

Because the Project 4 videotape database table has only a few entries, it will be easier to copy the information from the **Pam's Video Tapes** table to the new **Imported Video List** table. Before you do that, however, you must add to the new table all the fields contained in the existing **Pam's Video Tapes** table. With the **Imported Video List: Table** window still open, switch to the **Database** window and click the **Design** tool on the toolbar.

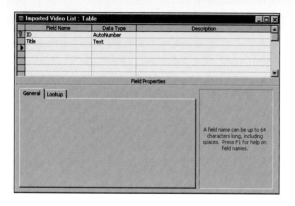

16 Add Fields to the New Table

In the **Table** window in Design view, add these fields to the **Imported Video List** table: Male Star (press **Tab** three times to leave the **Data Type** field set to the default **Text** and to leave the **Description** field blank), Female Star, Director, Type, Rating, Year (change the **Data Type** to Date/Time), Purchased (change the **Data Type** to Yes/No), and Notes (change the **Data Type** to Memo).

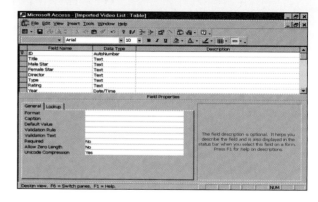

_17_ Copy Previous Data

In the **Database** window, double-click to open the **Pam's Video Tapes** table from Project 4 in Datasheet view. Place the cursor anywhere in the table. From the **Edit** menu, choose **Select All Records** (or press **Ctrl+A**). Also from the **Edit** menu, choose **Copy** (or press **Ctrl+C**).

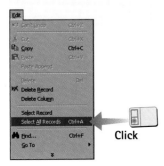

Click

_18_ Move to the Bottom of the Table

Switch back to the **Imported Video List** window in Datasheet view and place the cursor at the end of the table. You can move past the last record in the table by clicking the button at the bottom of the window that has both an arrow and an asterisk on it.

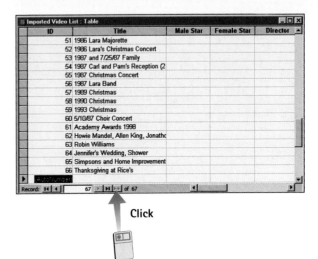

Click

_19_ Paste Append to New Table

From the **Edit** menu, click **Paste Append** to paste the records you copied from the **Pam's Video Tapes** table at the end of the **Imported Video List** table.

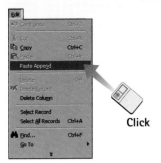

Click

Continues

How-To Hints

Moving Through the Records

You can move through the records in the **Table** window in several ways:

- ✓ Scroll manually through the list of records using the up-arrow and down-arrow keys on the keyboard.

- ✓ Scroll through the list one record at a time by clicking the single-arrow buttons at the bottom of the **Table** window.

- ✓ Jump to the first or last record in the list by clicking the arrow buttons with a stop-bar.

- ✓ Jump to the first new record at the end of the list (the record following the last record in the list) by clicking the arrow button with an asterisk.

Project 5 Continued

20 Answer Clippit

Clippit the Office Assistant asks you whether you're sure you want to paste these records. Click **Yes**.

Click

21 Adjust the Table

Close the **Pam's Video Tapes** table by clicking the **Close box** in the upper-right corner. In the **Imported Video List** window, make any adjustments you want to the field widths and save the table. You can cut and past to adjust some of the records, too.

ID	Title	Male Star	Female Star	Director
52	1986 Lara's Christmas Concert			
53	1987 and 7/25/87 Family			
54	1987 Carl and Pam's Reception (2			
55	1987 Christmas Concert			
56	1987 Lara Band			
57	1989 Christmas			
58	1990 Christmas			
59	1993 Christmas			
60	5/10/87 Choir Concert			
61	Academy Awards 1998			
62	Comedians: Allen King, Jonathon	Howie Mandel		
63	Comedian	Robin Williams		
64	Jennifer's Wedding, Shower			
65	Simpsons and Home Improvement			
66	Thanksgiving at Rice's			
67	Picture Perfect	Jay Mohr	Jennifer Aniston	Glen Gordon C
(AutoNumber)				

22 Delete the First Table

Because you moved all records (both of them!) to the new table, you no longer need the **Pam's Video Tapes** table. In the **Database** window, right-click the **Pam's Video Tapes** item and click **Delete**. (If the Office Assistant or a warning box asks whether you want to delete this table, click **Yes**.)

Right-click

How-To Hints

When in Doubt, Work from a Backup

Why work from a backup? Because after you've taken the time to create a table, you don't want to inadvertently delete data or make other changes that you can't "undo." Microsoft Access often automatically saves changes you make to your database without prompting you first. To read more about backing up your database, see Project 4, "Creating a Custom Form," and Part 3, Task 12, "How to Back Up a Database."

Change a Table Name

If you want, you can give your table a more meaningful name than **Imported Video List**: With **Tables** selected in the Objects bar, right-click the table name and choose **Rename**; type the new name to replace the old one. A caveat: Throughout this project, we'll still refer to this table as the **Imported Video List** table, regardless of how you change its name.

23 Oh, Look! An Inventory Database!

Oops! Now that you've created a videos table, notice that the **Inventory** sample database included with Access 2000 is for a *household inventory*. How convenient! You can link your videos table to a table in the **Inventory** database if you add another field to your videos table.

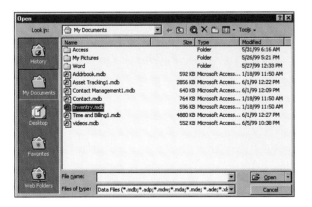

24 Add the Link Field

Switch to the **Imported Video List: Table** window in Design view. At the bottom of the list of fields in the top pane, type **CategoryName** as the new field name. Press **Tab** twice to set **Text** as the data type. In the **Description** column, type **Table linked to Our_Inventry household goods database** to remind you that this field is the link. Save the table and exit Access.

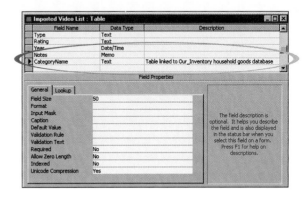

25 Find the Inventory Database

From the **Start** menu, choose **Programs, Windows Explorer**. Open the **My Documents** folder. From the **Tools** menu, select **Find, Files or Folders**. In the **Named** box of the **Find: All Files** dialog box, type **Inventry.mdb**. From the **Look in** drop-down menu, select **All hard drives**. Click **Find Now**.

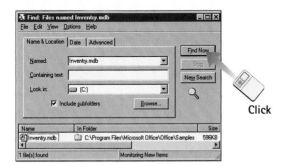

Click

26 Rename the Inventory File

When Windows finds the file, drag the file into your **My Documents** folder to copy it there. Now you can make all the changes you want to this copy without affecting the original database. Right-click the filename and select **Rename**. Change the name to **Our_Inventry.mdb**. Double-click the **Our_Inventry.mdb** icon to open the file in Access 2000.

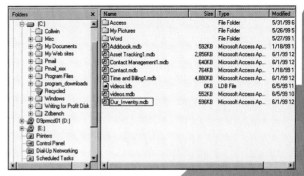

Continues

27 View the Inventory Database

Access opens the Household Inventory Main Switchboard. Minimize the Main Switchboard and maximize the **Our_Inventry: Database** window. In the Objects bar, select **Tables**. Double-click the **Categories** option in the **Objects** list. In the **Category Name** field, type **Video tape** at the bottom of the list. Click the **Close box** in the upper-right corner of the **Categories: Table** window.

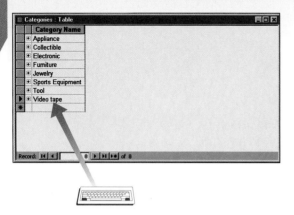

28 Link the Tables

Now you can link the **Imported Video List** table to the **Categories** table in this **Household Inventory** database. From the **File** menu, select **Get External Data, Link Tables**.

29 Select the Linkee

In the **Link** dialog box, select the database you want to link to the currently open database. In this case, the currently open database is **Our_Inventry.mdb**. The database that contains the information you want to link to the inventory is **videos.mdb**. Select this file and click **Link**.

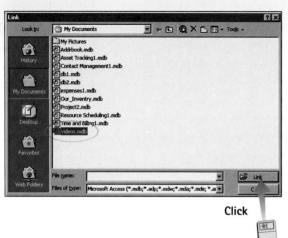

Click

30 Activate the Link

In the **Link Tables** dialog box, click **Imported Video List** to select that table as the one you want to link to the inventory database. Click **OK**.

Click

31 A New Table in the Objects List

The **Imported Video List** table now appears in the Objects list in the **Our_Inventry Database** window. To create a relationship between the two tables based on the **CategoryName** field, open the **Relationships** window, add the imported table, and create the new relationship.

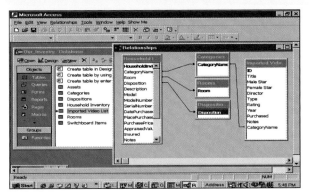

Whether you query the information in your database to determine the number of videos and other paraphernalia associated with Harrison Ford that reside in your collection (*Star Wars* memorabilia featuring Han Solo, *Indiana Jones* videos, and the like) or you simply want a printed "cheat sheet" of some of the details for a particular table, the Access 2000 Reports object is there to assist you. The next steps show you how to use the Reports feature.

Continues

How-To Hints

The Linked Advantage

Because a database can relate fields in tables that aren't necessarily contained in the same database file, changes made to one linked table automatically update the fields in another file. Linked fields save you from doing a tremendous amount of repetitious data entry.

This Is a Test

Now let's see the linked table at work. Close the **Our_Inventry** database file and open the **videos.mdb** file again. In the Objects bar, select **Tables**. Double-click **Imported Video List**. Type another video name at the end of the list (for example, type **This is a test**). Now close **videos.mdb** and open the **Our_Inventry** database again. Double-click the **Imported Video List** table in the **Database** window. *Ta-da!!!* Your new entry appears at the end of the list. From now on, you can make changes and additions to the **Imported Video List** table from either the **Our_Inventry** database or the **videos.mdb** database—and all the changes will appear in all the databases linked to the linked table.

32 Another Visit to the Wizard

Make sure that the **Our_Inventory** database is still open in Access 2000 and that the Database window is open. In the Objects bar, select **Reports** and double-click **Create report by using wizard**.

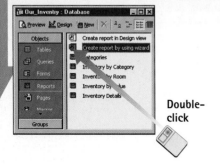

Double-click

33 Select the Fields for the Report

The **Report Wizard** dialog box asks you to determine which fields you want for your report. For this example, we want to generate a report that lists the categories in the **Our_Inventory** database. From the **Tables/Queries** drop-down list, select **Tables: Categories**. One field is displayed in the **Available Fields** pane: Select that field and click the > button to move it to the **Selected Fields** pane. Click **Next**.

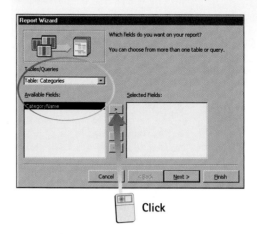

Click

34 Select the Sort Order

Although you can sort records using as many as four fields, in this example, we have only one field. From the drop-down list, select **CategoryName** and leave the default sort order (ascending—A to Z). Click **Next**.

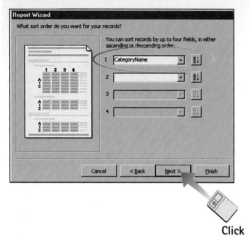

Click

35 The Report Layout

Specify how you want the report to look. Experiment with the options (we chose **Columnar** layout and **Portrait** orientation). Select the **Adjust the field width so all fields fit on a page** option and click **Next**.

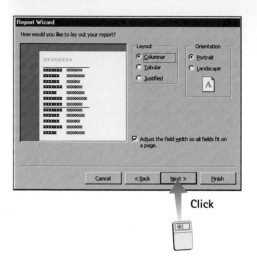

Click

36 You've Gotta Have Style

The Report Wizard then asks for you to choose the style of your report. Experiment with the options (we chose **Corporate**) and then click **Finish**.

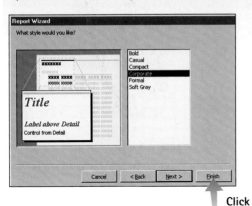

Click

37 Print Preview Your Report

Access 2000 opens the report in Print Preview mode. Click the **Print** button on the toolbar to send the report to the default printer. Although this report isn't too complicated, it gives you an idea of how succinctly Access reports can present complicated data.

Our Inventory Categories Report

Category Name	Appliance
Category Name	Collectible
Category Name	Electronic
Category Name	Furniture
Category Name	Jewelry
Category Name	Sports Equipment
Category Name	Tool
Category Name	Video tape

End

How-To Hints

The Report on Reports

Reports can be as complex or as simple as you make them. For more information on reports, see Part 7, "Creating Access Reports," or refer to *Using Microsoft Access 2000* (published by Que Corporation).

Task

Sharing Access Data with Other Programs and Users

*I*n today's fast-paced world, the ability to share information and share it quickly is vital to the success of any enterprise—be it a business, charitable, or personal endeavor. Access 2000 makes it easy to convert objects to what has quickly become the most universally accepted format: Web pages.

There will also be times when you want to share the data in an Access object with another application, such as Excel or Word. Other times, you may need to send the data to someone who uses another database and has to convert your Access data to his or her format. In this part of the book, you learn how to save your Access 2000 objects in those formats, as well as in formatted text (.RTF), unformatted text.

Because, in most cases, Access 2000 lets you save objects in HTML file format and retain your original object formatting, you have the assurance that anyone who has a browser (such as Microsoft Internet Explorer) can view the pages created from your Access 2000 objects and will see the pages with the appearance you intended them to have, either by opening the HTML file in the browser while offline (as you learn in Task 5) or by calling up a Web page or site while online.

As you learn in Task 7, Office 2000 makes it easy to publish your Access 2000 documents to your intranet or to an Internet site because the new File Open and File Save dialog box options make saving files to a Web server as simple as storing them on your hard disk or saving them to a file server.

By now, you know that your database as a whole has a filename with the extension .MDB; the database objects (tables, queries, forms, reports, and so on) are lumped up into that .MDB file; that is, the objects in your database clump together to form the entire database. As you learn in the following tasks, Access 2000 gives you the tools necessary to easily convert those objects or portions of an object to another format. ●

How to Save an Access Object in Another Format

There may be times when you want to use your Access data in an application such as Word or Excel. Other times, you only need to share the facts and figures—perhaps with someone who prefers to start from scratch when he or she formats a desktop publishing file—so an ASCII text file will suffice. For those times when your desktop publisher uses an antique computer and you're not certain which Word file formats will be compatible but you want to drop some subtle hints about how the final page output should appear, you can save your work as an .RTF file, which preserves your formatting. Access 2000 makes it easy to save your work in another format.

Begin

1 Select the Object

With your database open in Access and the **Database** window active, click the object you want to save in another format to highlight that object. In this example, the **Household Inventory** table has been selected.

Click

2 Start the Export Process

From the **File** menu, choose **Export**.

Click

3 Select Your Filepath

If you want to save the object to another filepath (a different folder or partition on your hard drive, for example), make that change by clicking the **Save in** control's drop-down list arrow and browsing to the desired folder.

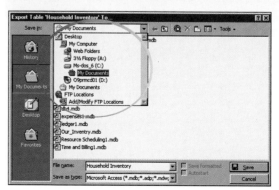

④ Specify the Filename

Type a filename for the object you are saving or use the name Access suggests. Access will add the appropriate extension automatically based on the option you select in the next step.

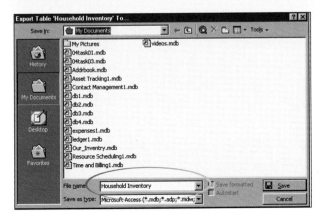

⑤ Select the Format

From the **Save as type** drop-down list, choose the format in which you want to save this object. For example, select **Excel**, **Word**, or **Text File** to save the object in a readily accessible format.

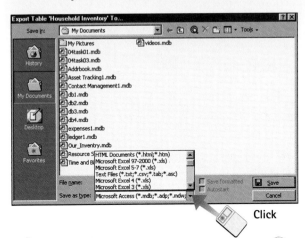

Click

⑥ Save Your Work

Select the **Save formatted** option if you want to save the object and keep its appearance similar to how it looks in Access. For example, you can save an Access table in Excel format, keeping the appearance (the fonts, point sizes, and so on) of the Access table. If you don't select this option, the data is saved using a standard text format. Note that not all objects can be saved with their Access appearances intact. Click **Save**.

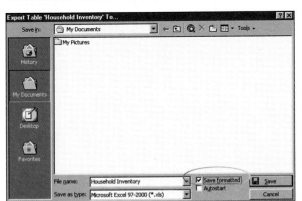

End

How-To Hints

Open an Object in Word

You can easily open an entire datasheet, form, or report in Word: In the **Database** window, select the object you want to load in Word. (If you only want to see a portion of the object, open it in Access and select the portion you want to view in Word.) From the Access menu, select **Tools, Office Links, Publish It with MS Word**. (You can access this option from the toolbar's **Office Links** button, too.) Access saves your data in Rich Text Format (.RTF) and automatically opens Word with that data displayed.

Filepath Foibles

When you export data from Access 2000, you are not creating an Access 2000 object. You're saving the information in whatever format you designate (such as an .HTML file). You may already have a foolproof system in place to ensure that you can find those exported files when you need them. One method that works for us is to create an folder within the My Documents folder. Inside the EXPORT folder, we add additional folders such as HTML, EXCEL, TEXT, RTF, and so on.

How to Save a Portion of an Access Object in Another Format

Access lets you save a selection for those times when you need to save only part of an object in another format. For example, you can save a portion of an Access table (rather than the entire thing) in another format.

Begin

1 Pick Your Part

With the database open and the **Database** window active, select the object you want to work with and click **Open** on the database toolbar. Select the portion of the object you want to save in another format.

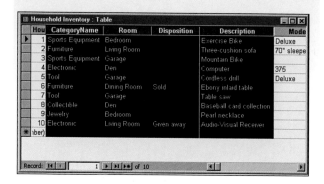

2 Export the Selection

From the **File** menu, choose **Export**.

Click

3 Change the Filepath

If you want to save the object to another filepath (a different folder or partition on your hard drive, for example), make that change by clicking the **Save in** control's drop-down list arrow and browsing to the desired folder.

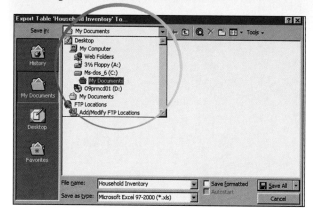

4 Specify the Filename

Type a filename for the object you are saving or use the name Access suggests. Access will add the appropriate extension automatically based on the option you select in the next step.

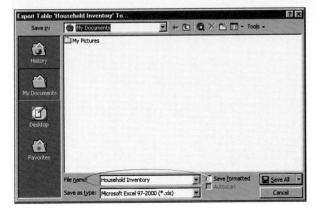

5 Select the Format

From the **Save as type** drop-down list, choose the format in which you want to save this object. For example, select **Excel**, **Word**, or **Text File** to save the object in a format that is readily accessible by these applications.

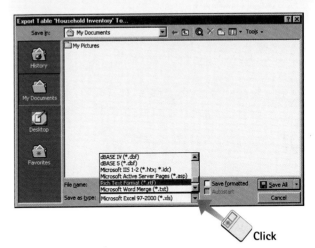

Click

6 Save the Selection

Select the **Save formatted** option if you want to save the object with its appearance similar to how it looks in Access. Click the arrow to the right of the **Save All** button to bring down the list of save options. Choose **Save Selection**.

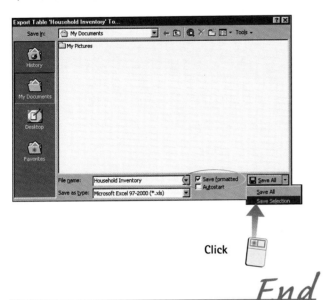

Click

How-To Hints

Getting a Grasp on the Logic of "Save Formatted"

Although somebody somewhere probably has the logic of the Save Formatted option down to an exact science, we've found that with most casual and business usage, you'll probably be doing some trial and error at first to determine which object conversions can and cannot use this feature. Based on our experience, there are times when Save Formatted is selected automatically (displayed as grayed out, yet with the check mark in front of it). Other times, the option just isn't available. In most cases, you can employ Save Formatted when you work with Excel 5-7, Excel 97-2000, Text file, and HTML format saves.

End

How to Create a Web Page from a Table, Query, or Form

In this day and age, sometimes the simplest way to display your data for others is to publish it to your intranet or on the Internet. Access lets you save a table, query, or form as a Web page.

Begin

1 Choose the Object to Export

With the database open and the **Database** window active, select the table, query, or form you want to save as a Web page.

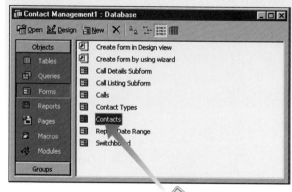

Click

2 Export to a Web Page

From the **File** menu, choose **Export**.

Click

3 Set the Filepath

If you want to save the object to another filepath (a different folder or partition on your hard drive, for example), make that change by clicking the **Save in** control's drop-down list arrow and browsing to the desired folder. Alternatively, you can select a folder by clicking one of the icons (**History, My Documents, Desktop,** or **Favorites**) on the Places bar.

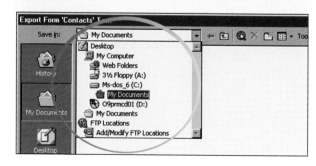

4 Name the Web Page

In the **File name** box, type the filename you want to use for your Web page.

5 Preserve the Page Appearance

In the **Save as type** box, choose **HTML Documents**. If it isn't already selected by default, select the **Save formatted** option if you want to save the page with an appearance similar to how it looks in Access.

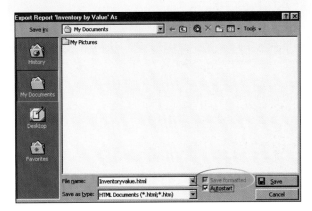

6 Save the Web Page

Click the **Save** button.

Click

End

How-To Hints

AutoStart

When you save a datasheet to a Web page, Access gives you the option of having it automatically display in your default Web browser after you click **Save**. Select the **AutoStart** option in the **Export** dialog box (available only when you save to HTML format and choose the **Save formatted** option) to activate this option.

Open an Object in Excel

You can easily open an entire datasheet, form, or report in Excel: In the Database window, select the object you want to work with. (If you want to move only a portion of the object, open it in Access and select the portion you want to view in Excel.) From the Access menu, select Tools, Office Links, Analyze It With MS Excel. (You can access this option from the toolbar's OfficeLinks button, too.) Access saves your data as a Microsoft Excel file (.XLS) in the default database folder and automatically opens Excel with that data displayed.

How to Create a Web Page from a Report

Unlike the single Web page you get when you save a datasheet table, query, or form in HTML format, you get sequentially numbered and linked Web pages (one file for each printed page) when you save a datasheet report in HTML format.

Begin

1 Choose the Object to Export

With the database open and the **Database** window active, select the report you want to save as a Web page.

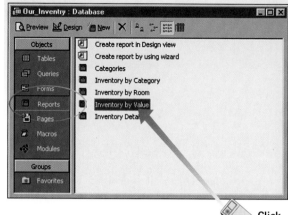

Click

2 Export to a Web Page

From the **File** menu, choose **Export**.

Click

3 Set the Filepath

If you want to save the object to another filepath (a different folder or partition on your hard drive, for example), make that change by clicking the **Save in** control's drop-down list arrow and browsing to the desired folder. Alternatively, you can select a folder by clicking one of the icons (**History, My Documents, Desktop,** or **Favorites**) on the Places bar.

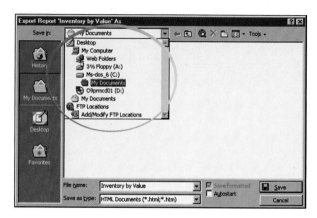

4 Name the Web Page

In the **File name** box, type the filename you want to use for your Web page. Keep in mind that Access will assign a numerical suffix to that filename for each page in your report.

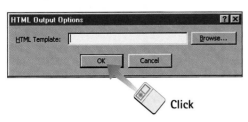

5 Preserve the Page Appearance

In the **Save as type** box, choose **HTML Documents**. If it isn't already selected by default, select the **Save formatted** option if you want to save the page with an appearance similar to how it looks in your Access report. Click the **AutoStart** option if you want to display the pages automatically in your default Web browser after you save them.

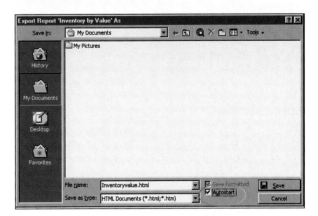

6 Save the Web Page

Click **Save**. Access gives you the opportunity to specify a template file that contains HTML tags and tokens that can be used to create a Web page with a specific navigation scheme. If you don't specify a template file, Access provides the hyperlinks necessary for navigation through the pages of the Web report. Click **OK**.

Click

End

How-To Hints

Encounters of the Web Page Kind

Each report has different quirks that make it impossible to describe every scenario you may encounter as you export reports to your Web pages. For instance:

✓ If your report contains a parameter query (see Part 5, "Working with Database Table Queries"), Access prompts you to input those values and then exports the results.

✓ Fields that already contain a hyperlink data type output as hyperlink addresses by using the `<a href>` HTML tag.

How to View Access Web Pages

It's always a good idea to preview your Web pages before publishing them to your Web site or to an intranet. To take a look at the Web pages you've created in the preceding tasks in Internet Explorer, follow these steps.

Begin

1 Open Internet Explorer

From the **Start** menu, choose **Programs**, **Internet Explorer**. (Windows 98 users can choose **Launch Internet Explorer** on the task bar.) If prompted, choose **Work Offline**.

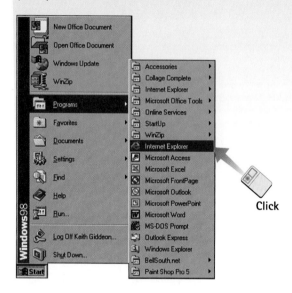

Click

2 Select File, Open

From the Internet Explorer **File** menu, choose **Open**.

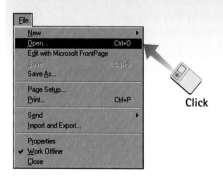

Click

3 Browse to Your File

Click **Browse** to look for the file of the Web page you want to preview. (If you know the Web page's filepath and filename, type it in the **Open** box.)

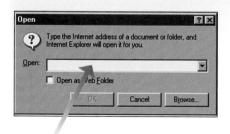

4 Select Your File

After browsing to the folder that contains the file for the Web page you want to open, click the filename. That filename appears in the **File name** box. Click **Open** to close the browsing dialog box.

Click

5 Open the File

The selected path and filename now appear in the **Open** dialog box. (The Open as Web Folder option is used when you want to specify that work can be done with files or folders on a Web server, such as a Microsoft FrontPage server. Check with your system administrator to see whether you have servers that are set up to work in this way.)Click **OK** to open the file.

Click

6 Preview the Web Page

You can now preview your Web page in Internet Explorer.

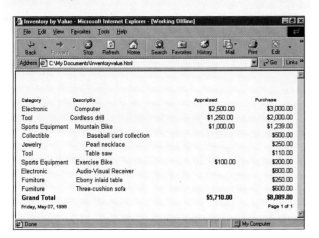

End

How-To Hints

Working Offline

You don't have to be online to preview a Web page—until you **publish** it to the Internet, the page resides on your hard drive only. Internet Explorer reads the file from your hard drive rather than retrieving it from a server. (See Task 6 for information on how to publish your site to the WWW or an intranet.) Remember that for your links to work and for your data to display properly, all the files associated with your Web pages (such as the sequential files created when you save a report as Web pages) must reside within the same folder on your hard drive. If you move one file to another folder or partition, the links from it to the other pages will be lost (and vice versa).

How to Attach a Database Object to Email

If you use Access long enough, you will eventually have to attach a database object to an email message. Maybe you'll have to send an Access report to a family member or a table of data to your boss across the country. In this example, you'll learn how to attach a report on your household inventory (from the our_inventry.mdb database) to an email message to your insurance agent.

Begin

1 Choose the Objects List

Open the our_inventry.mdb database so that the **Database** window appears. From the Objects bar, choose the type of object you want to send as an email attachment. For this example, choose **Reports**.

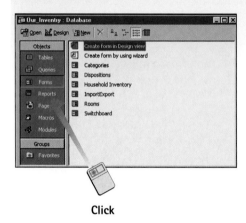

Click

2 Select the Object

From the Objects list, select the object you want to attach to your email message. For this example, select **Inventory by Value**.

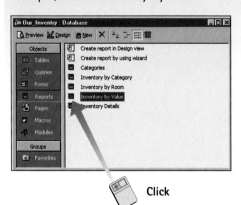

Click

3 Open the Send Dialog Box

Select **File, Send To, Mail Recipient (as Attachment)** to open the **Send** dialog box.

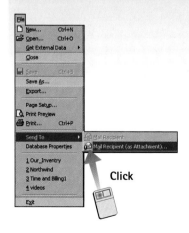

Click

4 Choose Attachment Format

In the **Send** dialog box, choose the format in which you want to send the attachment. For this example, choose **Rich Text Format**. Click **OK**.

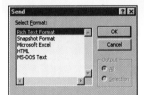

5 Address the Email

Enter the address(es) of the recipient(s) in the appropriate fields. If you want to address the message to more than one person in a field, separate the addresses with semicolons (;). Don't forget to enter a **Subject** line and some message text as well.

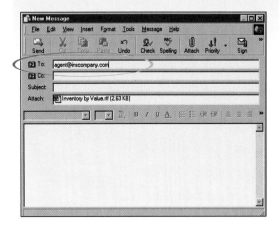

6 Send the Email

Click the **Send** button on the dialog box toolbar to send the message to all parties listed in the **To** and **Cc** fields.

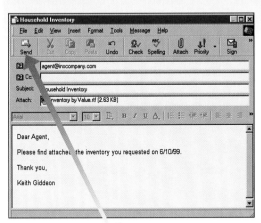

Click

How-To Hints

Double-Check Email Addresses!

For security reasons, be absolutely sure that you address your email messages correctly when you attach objects from your databases. You don't want your messages delivered to the inboxes of those whom you don't want to view the data attached.

End

How to Add an FTP Site to Access

The need to add File Transfer Protocol (FTP) sites to the Access dialog box system is inevitable. It seems that we're always adding domains or changing ISP accounts. If you intend to fully use the Web capabilities of Access 2000, you need to know how to add an FTP site to Access's **Open** and **Save As** dialog boxes.

Begin

1 Open the Open Dialog Box

Choose **File, Open** to display the **Open** dialog box.

Click

2 Select Add/Modify FTP Locations

Select **Add/Modify FTP Locations** from the **Look in** box at the top of the **Open** dialog box. This opens the **Add/Modify FTP Locations** dialog box.

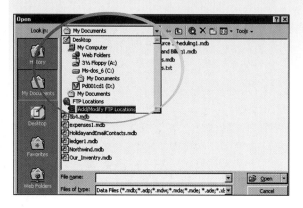

3 Enter the Site Name

In the **Name of FTP site** text box, type the site name you want to give the site you are adding. This name should include the server name for the FTP site, at the least. (For example, ftp.mysite.com. Access will add the ftp:// protocol.) The name you type here will appear in the **Open** dialog box's **Look in** pull-down menu.

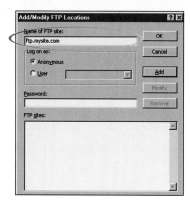

4 Enter the User Name

If you are not using an Anonymous login for the site specified in Step 3, click the **User** radio button. In the text box provided, enter the user name you typically use to access the site.

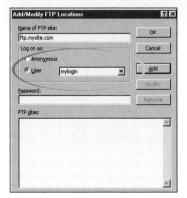

5 Enter the Password

In the **Password** box, type the password you typically use to access this FTP site. As you type, the password appears as asterisks in the text box, so make sure that you type the password correctly. Click **Add**. The site name appears in the **FTP Sites** box. Click **OK**.

6 Log on to the Site

When you need to log on to this FTP site, select **File**, **Open** and select the site name from the **Look in** pull-down menu.

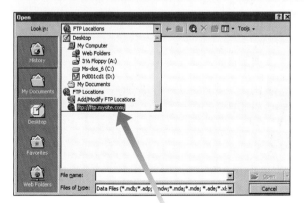

 Click

End

How-To Hints

Maintaining Your List of Sites

When an FTP site is outdated and won't be used again, be sure to remove it from the list. Do this by selecting **FTP Locations** in the **Open** dialog box's **Look in** pull-down menu. Right-click the FTP site name and select **Remove** from the shortcut menu.

File Transfer Protocol

FTP is simply a standard way of transferring a file from one location to another—usually to, from, or on the Internet.

Project 6

Using the Address Book in a Mail Merge

There are many times when you may want to send the same letter to a group of people, such as the dreaded Christmas or holidays family newsletter, information about a summer company get-together complete with directions to the picnic site, a fund-raising letter for a church or organization, and so on. Yet you want to personalize each letter, too. You can do so if you create a form letter and then *merge* it with data in your Access Address Book. In this project, you learn how to do this. You also learn how to create mailing labels and begin to modify the Address Book that comes with Access 2000 so that you can use it as your own.

1 Open Access

Open Access: From the **Start** menu, choose **Programs, Microsoft Access**.

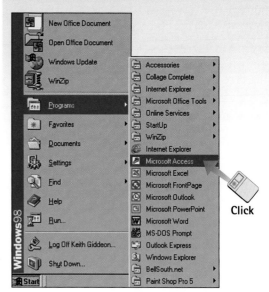

2 Open the Address Book in Access

You can find the addrbook.mdb file in the Office\Samples directory. From the Access **Startup** dialog box, select the **Open an existing file** option, locate the **ADDRBOOK** file in the **Samples** directory, and click **OK**. (Alternatively, select **ADDRBOOK** from the **Open** dialog box, if it's available.)

3 The Main Switchboard

The Address Book database opens with the **Main Switchboard** active. You're going to let Access help you create your mail merge document, so click **Merge It With Word**.

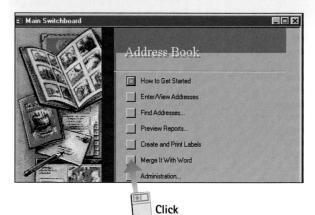

4 We're Off to See Another Wizard

The Microsoft Word Mail Merge Wizard opens. Click **Create a new document and then link data to it**. Click **OK**.

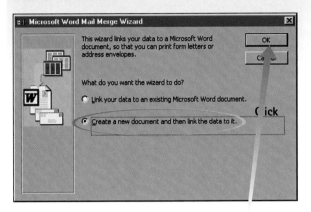

Click

5 Start Your Word Document

Access opens a blank document in Word with the **Mail Merge** toolbar active. In this document, type any letterhead-style information that may be necessary. (See the How-To Hint on this page if you're using letterhead stationery.)

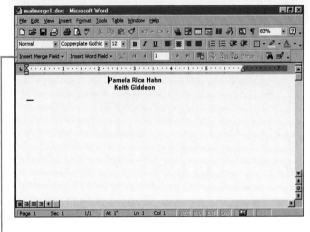

└─ Mail merge toolbar

6 Add the Fields

Press **Enter** to position the cursor on the page where you want to insert your field information. Select the **FirstName** field from the **Insert Merge Field** drop-down list. Notice that the list choices are the fields from the Address Book database.

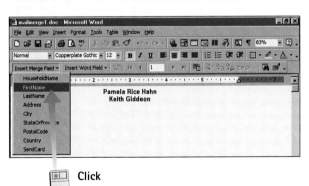

Click

Continues

How-To Hints

Merge Document Reminders

If you're using letterhead and need to make top-margin adjustments to accommodate the wording at the top of the page, you can do so from the Word menu. Choose **File, Page Setup**. To date your letter, choose **Insert, Date and Time** from the Word menu, choose your preferred format, and click **OK**.

Installing the Sample Databases

Can't find the sample database? Go to Access Help and search for the word *sample*. Choose **Sample databases included with Microsoft Access** from the options list. You'll see links to automatically install any of the sample databases provided with Access 2000. You may also want to make a backup copy of the database before you make substantial changes to it (backups are always a good idea).

7 Add Next Field

Press the **spacebar**, and then select the **LastName** field from the **Insert Merge Field** drop-down list. Press **Enter**.

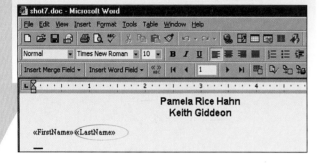

8 Add Remaining Fields

Add remaining merge fields and surrounding text. Be sure to insert any needed spacing or punctuation between your selected fields. (Don't be alarmed if the Office Assistant asks if you want help with your letter. He's there to offer support if you need it.)

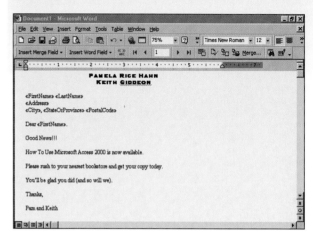

9 Save the Document

From the Word menu, select **File, Save As**. In the **File name** text box in the **Save As** dialog box, type the filename **merged_letter.doc** for the Word document you have just created and then click **Save**.

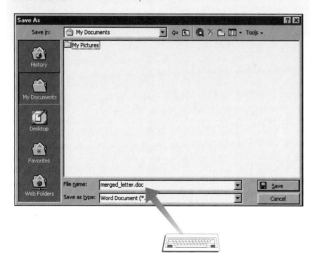

10 Select Tools, Mail Merge

Now you're ready to merge your letter with Access. This process inserts the field information from the database into the appropriate spots in the Word document. From the Word menu, select **Tools, Mail Merge**.

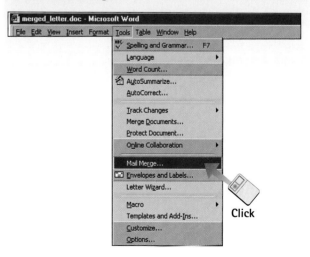

Click

11 The Mail Merge Helper

You've already created your main document (the Word file named merged_letter.doc) and selected your data source (the Access Address Book database). From the **Mail Merge Helper** dialog box, go to Step 3 and click **Merge**.

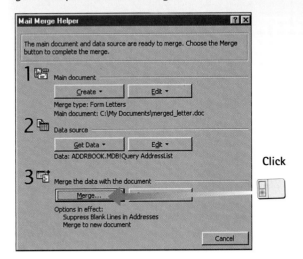

Click

12 The Merge Dialog Box

In the **Merge** dialog box, make sure that **New Document** appears in the **Merge to** box. Other options include merging to the printer, to email documents, or to fax documents.

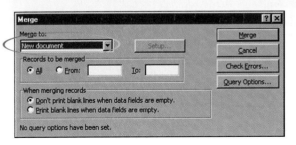

13 Check for Errors

Word and Access give you a chance to simulate the merge process so that you can check for errors. If you want to use this option, click the **Check Errors** button. In this example, however, you're ready to merge your letter, so click **Merge**.

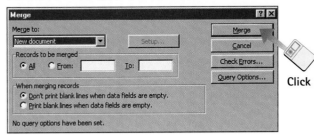

Click

Continues

How-To Hints

Query Options

You can set your query options from the **Merge** dialog box shown in Step 13. These options let you select or isolate specific Address Book records for your merge. Read more about queries in Part 5, "Working with Database Table Queries."

14 Look at the New Document

Word opens the resulting merged document in a new window. Notice that all the letters are in the same file, with a page break between each letter. Save your work with the filename final_merge.doc and exit Word.

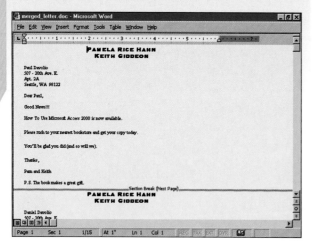

15 Create Mailing Labels

Now it's time to make some mailing labels for the form letters you just created. Return to the Address Book **Main Switchboard** and click **Create and Print Labels**.

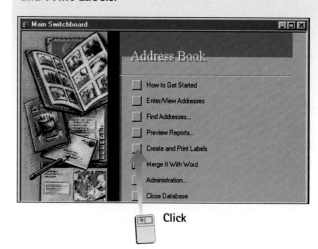

Click

16 Select the Label

In the **Label Wizard** dialog box, select the size of the labels you plan to use. From the **Filter by manufacturer** drop-down list box, select the name of the company that makes your labels. For this example, select **Avery**. Then click the appropriate units of measure, in this case **English**. Then select the actual label description, **5096**. Click **Next**.

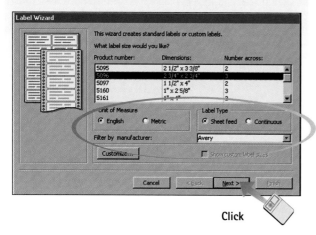

Click

17 Make Font Choices

From the drop-down list boxes, select the font, size, weight, and color of the text you want to print on the labels. Watch the sample text in the left pane to see the results of your selections. When you're satisfied, click **Next**.

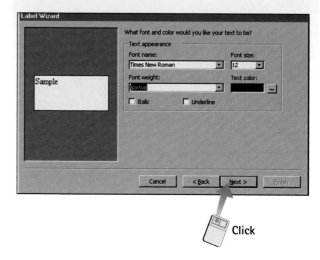

Click

18 Your Label Fields

The **Label Wizard** then asks what you would like on your mailing labels. Pick fields from the list box on the left (these fields are from the Address Book database) and click the **>** button. After each choice, make sure that you add necessary spacing, punctuation, and line feeds. You'll see your choices in the **Prototype label** box on the right. Click **Next**. You can also add optional text to appear on the label (such as **Have a Nice Day!**)

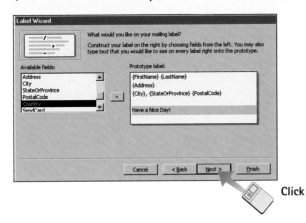

Click

19 Sort the Labels

You can sort the labels by the database fields. For example, you can sort the labels by last name and then by first name, or you can sort by ZIP code alone. (Note that if you select a database field that does not appear on the label, the sort is invalid.) Select from the available fields and click **Next**.

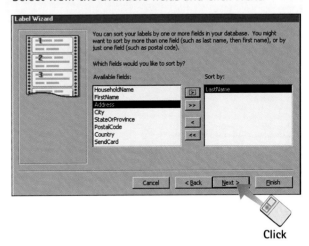

Click

20 Preview the Labels

Type a report name or keep the one the wizard assigns automatically. (This is the name that will appear in the **Database** window's Objects list when you click the **Reports** button.) Select the **See the labels as they will look printed** option and click **Finish**.

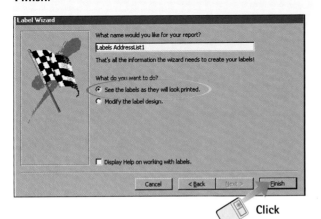

Click

How-To Hints

Labels, Labels, Labels

The Label Wizard has information about literally hundreds of labels from many manufacturers. If you don't see your manufacturer listed, or you don't see the exact product number of the labels you want to use, choose the closest match based on the dimensions and the numbers of labels across the page.

You Can Always Change Your Mind

If you don't like the appearance of the labels in Print Preview (Step 20), close the report document and restart the wizard (repeat Steps 15 through 20) to make any changes.

Continues

21 Print the Mailing Labels

Access displays the resulting mailing labels in Print Preview. If you're pleased with the result, select **File, Print**. You can open this list of labels at any time from the **Database** window by clicking the **Reports** button and selecting the report name you assigned to the list in Step 20.

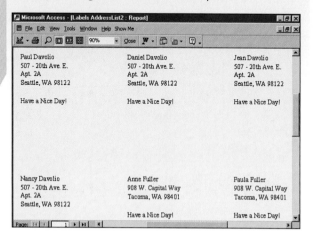

22 Make Changes to the Address

Now that you're familiar with the mail-merge process, take some time to learn your way around your Address Book. Return to the **Main Switchboard** and click **Enter/View Addresses**.

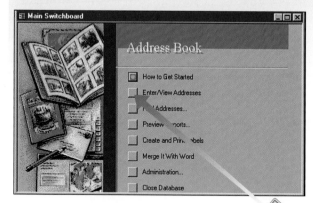

Click

23 View the Addresses

The Address Book opens in Form view. You can use this form to enter new information into the Address Book. However, because you want to delete all the existing (sample) records in this database before you enter your own data, you must first switch views. The Datasheet view provides the quickest and easiest way to delete records (as you see in Steps 25 and 26). Click the **Datasheet View** button at the bottom of the window.

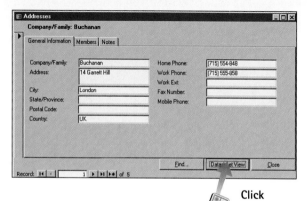

Click

24 Select Datasheet Display Fields

In the **Datasheet Display Fields** dialog box, choose the fields to be shown in Datasheet view. Because we're going to delete the existing records, select all the fields and then click **OK**.

25 Change the Datasheet View

Thanks to the underlying code in the Address Book database, you have just completed a select query without realizing it! Look around to become familiar with the fields in the Address Book. Chances are you don't know those people, so open the **Edit** menu and click **Select All Records**.

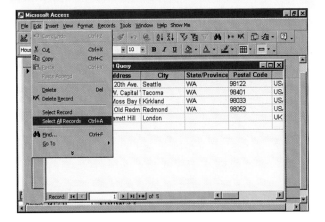

26 Delete the Records

Select **Edit, Delete Record**. (This action deletes all the records from the Address Book. It's okay to tell the Office Assistant yes if it gets nosy and asks whether you really want to delete these records. If you have hidden the Office Assistant, choose Yes at the dialog-box prompt.)

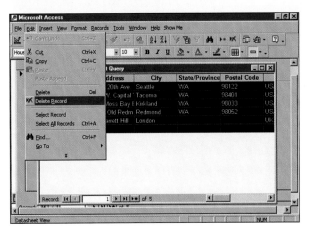

27 Enter Friends and Family

You're now ready to add your name and address data to the Address Book.

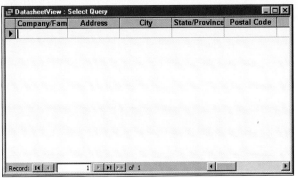

End

How-To Hints

Back Up and Then Back Up Again

As you work with Access 2000, you'll develop "backup habits" that work best for you. Until that time, consider doing this:

✓ Create an **Access Backup** folder in your **My Documents** folder. Before you start each Access session, paste a copy of the database on which you intend to work into the Backup folder.

✓ You may want to rename the file in the Backup folder to reflect the revision date.

✓ If an oops! makes it necessary to replace the current file with your backup copy, you can then delete the file in your **My Documents** folder, paste the backup file in its place, and rename the backup with the original filename.

Term at Top of Page

Glossary

append query   A query that adds a group of records from one or more tables to the end of one or more tables. Fields can be appended based on chosen criteria. You can also use an append query when you want to insert records with fields that don't match those fields in the table to which you are moving the data. In such instances, the append query appends data in the fields that match and ignores the other fields.

crosstab query   This type of query summarizes data by performing calculations on groups of data. For the most part, a crosstab query categorizes summarized data facts or groups of data, such as a total or average. For instance, if you want to view the monthly orders for a particular product for a portion of your customers or for all of them, a crosstab query is your best choice.

datasheet   A spreadsheet-style document that stores data in Access. Also called a *table*.

Datasheet view   In the Objects bar of the **Database** window, click **Tables**. In the Objects list, double-click a table to view the information in Datasheet view. In Datasheet view, you see all the records in a row and column format and often have to scroll sideways to look at them all.

data type   When you're creating fields in a database table, you can limit the kind of data that can be entered in each field by assigning a data type to the field. For example, if you assign the **Number** data type to a field, you can only enter numeric data in that field; you cannot enter text. Data types help keep the information that is entered in a field appropriate for that field.

delete query   A query that makes changes to records by deleting them from one or more tables. A delete query always deletes the entire record, not just selected fields within that record.

delimited file   A text file in which the various pieces of information are separated into columns by tabs, commas, or some other consistent character. For example, in a table created in Microsoft Word or a spreadsheet created in Excel, the data in the columns are separated by tab characters.

expression   The part of some Access operations that consists of identifiers (the elements that refer to the value of a field), operators (symbols such as < or words such as **Or** that indicate the operation to be performed), and values that produce a result.

field   An Access 2000 table stores each fact in a field (column).

filepath   The path from the root folder on a disk drive or hard drive partition to a particular file. For example, the familiar designation `C:\Desktop\My Documents\Household_Inventory.mdb` is a filepath to a single file.

fixed-width file   A text file in which the various pieces of information are separated into columns by spaces. For example, for a newspaper table that you have scanned and converted to a text file, the data in the columns is separated by spaces. A Microsoft Word or Excel file that has only a single column of data is also considered a fixed-width file. To import data from such a file into Access, make certain that the numbers and types of fields (columns) match those in the Access table.

form   The area in which you can enter, edit, and view table information one record at a time. Although you don't have to use a form to enter data into a database table, using a form is the easiest way to enter or edit data because it is in a fill-in-the-blank format.

Form view   In the Objects bar of the Database window, click **Forms**. In the Objects list, double-click a form to view the database table in Form view. In Form view, you see one record at a time.

G

group level   Sometimes referred to as a *break level*, the group level is the extent to which a group in a report or data access page is nested inside other groups. Groups result when a set of records associated by more than one field, expression, or group record source are nested. Beginning with level 0 (zero) as the first field, expression, or group record source on which you can sort or group, you can create up to 10 group levels in a report. There are no limits to the number of group levels in a data access page. Think of group levels as giving an Access report an indented outline appearance.

I

import   To place a *copy* of a file (or portion of a file) in another file. Changes you make to the copy do not affect the original file; changes you make to the original file are not reflected in the copy.

index   In a table, you can select fields you want Access to pay special attention to. The data you enter in these selected fields is indexed (much like the index at the end of a book) to facilitate later searches or queries through the table. A good field to select for an index is one you frequently refer to in searches or queries *and* that contains mostly unique data (such as a **Last Name** field would contain). Although you can index multiple fields in a table, be aware that the more fields you index, the more work Access has to do in the background to keep track of the data, and the less efficient the table may be in data-entry mode.

input mask   A filter that controls the kind of data that is entered into a table. For example, if you attempt to enter data the wrong way (such as all caps instead of lowercase letters), the input mask prevents you from doing so.

L

link   To place a *live copy* of a file (or portion of a file) in another file. The copy is *live* because it is connected to the original file by an electronic link. Changes you make to the original appear also in the copy; changes you make to the copy appear also in the original.

M

macro   A stored action or set of actions used to automate tasks.

mail merge   The process by which the data in fields in a database can appear in another document, customizing or personalizing the document.

For example, you can mail-merge an address database with a letter in Microsoft Word. In the multiple letters that result, each letter is customized with information from one record from the database.

make-table query   A query that creates a new table from data in one or more tables of a database.

many-to-many relationship   A relationship in which the linking values appear in numerous records in both tables.

module   A collection of Visual Basic for Applications files stored as a unit to direct declarations and procedures.

object (database)   The database objects in Microsoft Access 2000 are tables, queries, forms, reports, macros, and modules.

one-to-many relationship   A relationship in which the linking value in one table links to more than one record in other table, but a record in the second table can have only one matching record in the first table.

one-to-one relationship   A relationship in which there is only one record in each table that links the tables. For example, in the **Project2** database, only the **ContactID** field links the **Contacts** and **Calls** tables.

page   Access lets you export the data in a table, query, form, or report to a Hypertext Markup Language (HTML) file (Web page format) so that it can be viewed in Internet Explorer and other Web browsers.

parameter query   This type of query is useful when the criteria you want to use to filter the result set frequently changes. When you open a parameter query, it displays a dialog box into which you enter the parameters. The matching records then appear in Datasheet view.

Performance Analyzer   A component in Microsoft Access 2000 that can assess an entire database, or selected objects within a database, to determine and then advise of changes to make to optimize the database performance.

primary key   One or more fields in a database table, the values of which uniquely identify each record in the table. The primary key is also used to define the relationship of one table to another table or tables in the database.

query   A query is the way you ask Access questions about your database or alter the information in the database. It's a request for Access to search through multiple tables of a single database to locate records that meet a set of user-specified criteria.

query table   A table created to display the results of a query.

relationship   An established association between common fields (columns) in a database.

report   A summary of some aspect of your data that is intended to be printed. Access applies the word *report* to some unusual aspects of the database. For example, when you create a list of mailing labels, Access calls the resulting document a *report*.

result set   The table that Access creates as the result of a query. The table shows only those fields you have specified in the query.

$$S$$

select query   The most prevalent kind of query. It displays in Datasheet view the results of data pulled from one or more tables. A select query can be used to group records or to perform calculations, including (but not limited to) sums, counts, and totals. Also called a *simple query*.

sort In a report, the process by which records are organized in a particular order. Sorts are either *ascending* (from 0 to 9 and from A to Z) or *descending* (from 9 to 0 and from Z to A).

T

table The part of a database that consists of fields (columns) that store details about a class of information or facts. Each table consists of *fields* (columns) of data. A collection of fields (a row) makes up a *record*. A single database can contain more than one table, and those tables can have relationships to one another. A table is also called a *datasheet* in Access.

table relationships (relational database) A relational database is created when tables relate on a common field and those fields adhere to normalization rules. Using a link defined by a common field that appears in each table, a relationship established between those tables provides a way to avoid data repetition. Data stored in one table can be used (linked) to provide relevant data for a field in another table, such as complete customer information held in a table that's linked to the customer number reference used in another table.

U

update query A query that makes changes to data in selected existing records in one or more tables.

Index

Get FREE books and more...when you register this book online for our Personal Bookshelf Program

http://register.samspublishing.com/

SAMS

 Register online and you can sign up for our *FREE Personal Bookshelf Program*...unlimited access to the electronic version of more than 200 complete computer books—immediately! That means you'll have 100,000 pages of valuable information onscreen, at your fingertips!

 Plus, you can access product support, including complimentary downloads, technical support files, book-focused links, companion Web sites, author sites, and more!

 And you'll be automatically registered to receive a *FREE subscription to our weekly email newsletter* to help you stay current with news, announcements, sample book chapters, and special events, including sweepstakes, contests, and various product giveaways!

 We value your comments! Best of all, the entire registration process takes only a few minutes to complete, so go online and get the greatest value going— absolutely FREE!

Don't Miss Out On This Great Opportunity!

Sams is a brand of Macmillan Computer Publishing USA. For more information, please visit *www.mcp.com*

How to Use *provides easy, visual information in a proven, step-by-step format. This amazing guide uses colorful illustrations and clear explanations to get you the results you need.*

Other How to Use Titles

Microsoft Word 2000
Sherry Kinkoph
ISBN: 0-672-31531-9
$24.99 US/$37.95 CAN

Microsoft Excel 2000
Dan and Sandy Gookin
ISBN: 0-672-31538-6
$24.99 US/$37.95 CAN

Microsoft Outlook 2000
Dave Johnson
ISBN: 0-672-31588-2
$24.99 US/$37.95 CAN

Microsoft PowerPoint 2000
Susan Daffron
ISBN: 0-672-31529-7
$24.99 US/$37.95 CAN

Microsoft Access 2000
Jacqueline Okwudli
ISBN: 0-672-31491-6
$24.99 US/$37.95 CAN

Microsoft Windows 98
Doug Hergert
ISBN: 1-56276-572-8
$24.99 US/$37.95 CAN

America Online 4
Elaine Madison and Deborah Craig
ISBN: 1-56276-543-4
$24.99 US/$37.95 CAN

How to Use Computers
Lisa Biow
ISBN: 0-7897-1645-3
$24.99 US/$37.95 CAN

The Internet
Mark Walker
ISBN: 1-56276-560-4
$24.99 US/$37.95 CAN

SAMS

www.samspublishing.com

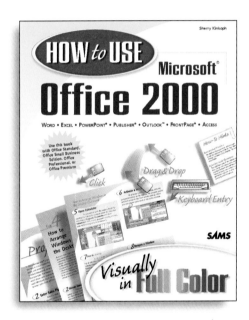

Microsoft Office 2000

Sherry Kinkoph
ISBN: 0-672-31522-X
$24.99 US/$37.95 CAN

All prices are subject to change.